D1385495

IRISH RUGBY SCRAPBOOK

IRISH RUGBY
SCRAPBOOK

Edmund Van Esbeck

PICTORIAL PRESENTATIONS
SOUVENIR PRESS

First published 1982 by Souvenir Press Ltd,
43 Great Russell Street, London WC1B 3PA
and simultaneously in Canada

ISBN 0 285 62545 4 casebound
ISBN 0 285 62546 2 paperback

Photoset and printed in Great Britain by
Photobooks (Bristol) Limited
Barton Manor, St Philips, Bristol

CONTENTS

ACKNOWLEDGMENTS

The research for this book was no onerous responsibility as I have lived through the period covered in the pages that follow.

It has been my great joy and pleasure to see most of the matches in the post war era in which Ireland has been involved and to know so many of the men whose deeds are central to the theme.

I would like to thank Ciaran Fitzgerald, the man who led Ireland to the Triple Crown and Championship in 1982, Willie John McBride who captained Ireland to win the International Championship in 1974 and Karl Mullen, the man who led Ireland in the most fertile period from 1948 to 1951.

I would also like to express my thanks to the Editor and Sports Editor of the *Irish Times* for permission to reproduce the photographs, and in particular to Mr. Peter Thursfield, of the *Irish Times* photographic staff.

Finally I would like to express my thanks to my wife Mary and the members of my family for their help and assistance and—of course their patience.

Edmund Van Esbeck
May 1982

PROLOGUE

An early history of rugby football, penned in the closing years of the last century, presented the theory that organised rugby in Ireland began with a split. It is true that two administrative bodies were set up in Ireland in 1874, but while a division would add a nice 'Irish' dimension to fit in with the widely held belief that the Irish are an unpredictable lot who love a fight, in fact the administrations, one based in Dublin and one in Belfast, owed nothing to a difference of opinion, or indeed of objectives. From the outset there was a unity of purpose, and every side to take the field since Ireland first entered the field of international rugby competition at the Oval, Kennington, against England, in 1875, has represented the whole of Ireland. The Irish Football Union and the Northern Football Union amalgamated under the one banner, the I.R.F.U., in 1879, and when the grey clouds gathered, as gather they did at times, through good days and through bad, rugby has been a shining example of what can be achieved in Ireland when the will and the spirit are coordinated in the cause of good.

It was students at Trinity College in Dublin who first played the specific and defined art form of football that we now know as rugby. The Trinity club was formed in 1854 and thus can claim to be the second oldest club in the world, pre-dated only by Guy's Hospital. It was on a Trinity initiative that the Irish Football Union was founded, so the debt owed to those pioneers of long ago is incalculable. The influence, too, of boys who had attended rugby playing schools in England was considerable in Trinity and two of them, Barrington and Wall, drew up a set of laws in 1866 that approximated in very close detail to a set that had been in operation in England.

Irish rugby, in the early years, was not often good, seldom great but soon had its own identifiable characteristics; many of them remain good to this day, not least the tremendous goodwill from outsiders, based on the ability to win and to lose with dignity.

It was not, for instance, until 1881 that Ireland won a match for the first time, when Scotland was beaten in Belfast. It was not until 1880 that Ireland scored a try, the distinction going to one J. Loftus Cuppidge, whose feat sent some of the scribes of the day into raptures.

In the period between 1875 and 1939, Ireland's ratio of success was meagre enough, yet they knew days of glory too. The Triple Crown was won for the first time in 1894 and the second in 1899. There would be a protracted wait until that mythical and elusive target was reached again.

In that time, Ireland won the International Championship just four times, but were foiled by Wales at the final hurdle in crown and championship on no fewer than seven occasions.

Although this book deals basically with the period since the resumption of the Championship in 1947, it is right, I believe, that we sketch the happenings in the earlier years and pay tribute to the men who fashioned the Irish rugby traditions.

From the outset, the Irish contributed handsomely to the development of the game and its administration. Indeed it was on an Irish initiative that the International Board was formed, a body elected to be the game's supreme ruling authority and formed in the aftermath of some contentious issues that did not involve the Irish.

Through the years, many Irishmen have contributed much to the Board, and no fewer than four Irishmen have held the office of honorary secretary: Eddie McAlister, R. G. Warren, Harry Thrift and Eddie Kirwan. Indeed that onerous position was an Irish preserve for almost three quarters of a century, its own vote of confidence in the calibre of the men who officiated.

Several others left an indelible imprint on the Board's workings, notably R. G. Warren, on the Board from 1887 to 1938, and more recently Sarsfield Hogan, who gave a quarter of a century of magnificent service.

From the outset, whatever the collective failings and the modest nature of the team achievement, a steady stream of great players and characters wore the green jersey of Ireland and, even in an era when communications were limited, still managed to gain recognition and admiration throughout the rugby world. Today one can sit in a room in Auckland and watch events unfold in a rugby international at Lansdowne Road, Twickenham and the other great stadia of the world. Not so before the last world war—such are the wonders of T.V.

It was an Irishman, George Stephenson, who held the world record for the number of caps won when international rugby was called to a summary halt in

The first Ireland rugby team ever to take to the field, against England at The Oval, Kennington, in 1875. The captain of the side was George Hall Stack from Trinity College, who provided the inspiration for the setting-up of the first administrative body for the game in Ireland.

1939. Stephenson, a threequarter of great skill, won 42 caps between 1921 and 1930, a magnificent achievement bearing in mind that the number of matches played then was very much smaller than today when tours are so prolific. There were many, however, who had come before Stephenson. One thinks of the great Louis Magee, who led Ireland to the Triple Crown in 1899 and who brought a new dimension to half back play; J. C. Parke and Fred Gardiner, Alf Tedford, and Basil Maclear, the man rejected by England on the grounds that he was not deemed good enough and then gladly claimed by Ireland with whom he reached the summit; Dickie Lloyd, George Hamlet, Mark Sugden, who became a scrum half by chance and brought to the position a new concept and a dummy of legendary proportions; Jammie Clinch, an incomparable character and a wing forward of courage, tenacity and, legend has it,

The Irish team which won the Triple Crown for the first time in 1894. Back row (l. to r.): James Lyttle, T. Crean, H. Lindsay, R. Garrett (President I.R.F.U.), C. V. Rooke, W. S. Brown, L. H. Gwynn, E. McAlister. Middle row (l. to r.): H. Wells, W. Gardiner, E. Forrest (capt.), J. O'Conor, S. Lee. Front row (l. to r.): B. Tuke, G. Walmsley, W. Sparrow, John Lyttle.

The Ireland team that beat Wales in Cardiff in 1899 to win the Triple Crown for the second time. Back row (l. to r.): W. Byron, M. Ryan, J. Sealy, J. Ryan, C. Moriarty, A. Meares. Seated (l. to r.): J. McIlwaine, E. Campbell, J. M. Lyttle, L. Magee (capt.), G. Allen, C. Reid, J. Harman. In front (l. to r.): G. P. Doran, P. O'Brien-Butler.

verbosity; Eugene Davy, who once scored three tries against Scotland in a blistering 20 minute spell; Paul Murray, capped in three different positions for Ireland behind the scrum. C. E. Allen and George Morgan, too, are names secure forever in the annals of the rugby game.

Prior to 1939, a host of Irishmen had represented the Lions and two, Tom Smyth (1910) and Sammy Walker (1938) led the Lions in South Africa. They certainly set a trend to be followed later.

This book is basically concerned with Irish rugby from the resumption of the International Championship series in 1947 to the present day, but I think it appropriate, in order that we may appreciate more readily the essence of Irish rugby, that the background be put in perspective. The rugby playing schools of Ireland have sent forth a steady flow of players, and if in numerical terms the number of schools has been relatively small, the number grows apace now as the game spreads. When the first administrative body was set up in Ireland over a century ago, its members set as their goal the promotion and fostering of the game of rugby football in Ireland; they have succeeded admirably in that objective.

It is no one's right to impose on history an ideal that might have been; rather it is his responsibility to interpret events supported by evidence. I hope the pages that follow are in accord with that worthy precept.

With a fine disregard for the laws of the game as they then applied, William Webb Ellis took the ball in his hands and ran with it. In Ireland they have been doing that for a long time now. The ancient Irish game of Caid had many similarities with rugby football and I think it true that the nature of the game appeals greatly to the Irish character and temperament. Over the last 35 years Ireland has known success and disappointment on the rugby field; here I endeavour to bring to life the history of the game in Ireland during that period. A history I have lived through, much of which I have seen played out on home ground and on foreign fields.

(Right) Con Murphy, the only Ireland player to win caps before and after the Second World War, presents members of the Ireland team to the President of Ireland, Sean T. O'Kelly, prior to one of the Victory Internationals at Lansdowne Road in 1945.

THE GREATEST ERA

WHEN THE worst and most destructive conflagration in the history of mankind finally ended in 1945 and the dreadful call of war no longer sounded for youth, sport eventually got back onto a normal basis. Indeed, not surprisingly after six years of austerity, people sought relaxation, and attendances at sporting fixtures reached a peak.

International rugby had ceased at the end of the 1939 championship, and, while there were a few services internationals, and while the game was played a lot in the services, in Britain the whole scene was badly disrupted.

The club scene in Ireland was not adversely affected by the war, and of course the schools

The Ireland team that won the Triple Crown (Ireland's third Triple Crown triumph, and the first won on Irish soil), the International Championship and performed Ireland's only Grand Slam to date, in 1948. Back row (l. to r.): Ernie Crawford (I.R.F.U. touch judge), W. D. McKee, J. McCarthy, J. C. Daly, J. Nelson, C. Callan, D. O'Brien, W. McKay, B. O'Hanlon, M. Allen (referee). Seated (l. to r.): A. McConnell, B. Mullan, K. Mullen (capt.), Dr. T. McGrath (President I.R.F.U.), D. Higgins, P. Reid. In front: E. Strathdee, J. Kyle. Insets: J. Mattsson, M. O'Flanagan, D. de Lacy.

17

Ireland's most successful captain, Karl Mullen, presents his players to Earl Granville, the Governor of Northern Ireland, prior to the 1948 Triple Crown match against Wales in Belfast.

continued to contest the provincial cup competitions and the provinces of Leinster, Munster, Ulster and Connacht met on a regular basis.

In addition, a very good fixture was added to the rugby calendar when, in 1942, an Irish XV met the British Combined Services in Belfast and that fixture was established for the duration of the war. It was to prove extremely valuable to Ireland in that it gave representative experience to the young talented players, who would, in ordinary circumstances, have been contesting for full international caps.

Yet when in 1946 a series of 'victory' internationals was arranged between the four Home countries and France, the long valley period was reflected in the fact that when Ireland met France in Dublin, only three men who had played for Ireland in the pre-war period were still on hand: Con Murphy, a full back from the Lansdowne club, wing Fred Moran from Clontarf, and forward Dave O'Loughlin from the Dolphin club in Cork.

Suggestions that Europe had been on starvation diet were certainly given the lie, were one to judge by the physical attributes of the French side, who had two particular giants in the second row pair, Soro

and Moga. France won the game and indeed Ireland was to be whitewashed that season, losing all four matches.

There were some youngsters in the side nonetheless whose talent was obvious and in this regard, none was more impressive than a young medical student from the Queen's University club, John Wilson Kyle, who was at outside half in the four matches.

In the middle of the front row a young hooker from the Old Belvedere club had looked impressive. Karl Mullen's name then meant little to the great mass of rugby enthusiasts; he was later to leave an indelible mark on the world scene.

The following season in 1947, it was back to normal when the International Championship and Triple Crown series were resumed and France, who had dropped out of the championship in 1931 after suggestions of professionalism and allegations about foul play and loose administration, were back on the scene. It was obvious that their protracted period in the wilderness had not been wasted.

Once more the French presented the opening challenge to Ireland in Dublin and won by 12–8, not a happy beginning for the Irish. For the French,

During the match Des O'Brien, Ireland's number eight, breaks through the Welsh defence, supported by second row Jimmy Nelson.

Jim McCarthy scores the try that gave Ireland the Triple Crown and the Championship against Wales at St. Helen's, Swansea, in 1949.

however, things could scarcely have been better, as they had beaten Scotland and so stood at the summit of affairs. Con Murphy was the only player to survive from the pre-war national side.

Even in defeat, however, it was apparent that Ireland had the nucleus of a good pack of forwards; they had the talents of Kyle at out half, and as events unfolded, it was to be the pack and the incomparable

Kyle who would steer Ireland to unprecedented heights of glory. But some work, and some frustration, still lay ahead.

The defeat by France did not bring much alteration to the Irish side. In the pack Mullen was propped by a fine player from Ulster in M. R. Neely and by John Christopher Daly, a man who had fought the good fight in the war. The second row was manned by the ample figures of Colm Callan and Bob Agar, from Malone, and in the back row too there was quality, but as yet not the unity later to play so important a part in the strategy of the side.

Bertie O'Hanlon, from the Dolphin club in Cork,

was brought into the side for the game against England and Murphy was still at fullback. There followed a quite remarkable performance in which the English were devastated by 22 points to nil. Never before or since has so convincing a win been attained by the Irish against the 'Old Enemy'.

Oddly, one victim of that match was Con Murphy, who was dropped even though he was captain, and the leadership passed to J. D. Monteith who played in the centre. Ireland beat Scotland readily enough at Murrayfield to set up the Triple Crown chance against Wales in Swansea. Not since 1889 had Ireland won at Swansea, an intimidating statistic as the players prepared for the task ahead.

One new cap was named for the game, Mick Lane, who, although a wing threequarter with the University Colle Cork club, was placed in the centre, a hazardous role bearing in mind the quality of the opposition.

Once more Ireland lost to Wales at St. Helen's and, although the margin was narrow enough, the skills of the great Haydn Tanner at scrum half for Wales proved too much and Ireland lost 6-0. It was the fifth time since 1930 that Wales had foiled the Irish at the final Triple Crown hurdle.

The Australians came to Britain and Ireland in the autumn of 1947. It was appropriate that it should be the Wallabies who were first to resume the touring schedule, as they had come to Britain in the autumn of 1939 and had had to return home without playing.

There was no joy for Ireland when they met the Australians at Lansdowne Road in a game that saw Ireland play Kevin O'Flanagan on the wing. O'Flanagan was a sportsman of the most rounded skills. He was an international soccer player who saw service with Arsenal and Brentford, he was an Irish sprint and long jump champion and he also found time to qualify as a medical doctor.

Ireland lost to Australia by 16-3, not a very good omen for the forthcoming championship tests and the visit to Paris, scheduled for New Year's day 1948.

If Ireland travelled to France as outsiders, they defied the odds and once again gave substance to the belief that the Irish always do best when least expected.

When the team to meet France was named, a new cap came in on the flank. Jim McCarthy, from Dolphin, would be a central figure in later events and proved a tremendous ally to Kyle in the tactical ploys of the Irish side. Those tactics had to disguise what was basically a limitation in the centre, but there were good wings on hand in Barney Mullan from Clontarf, and in O'Hanlon. At full back

Dudley Higgins, from the Civil Service club in Belfast, was now established. The back row was a key area with McCarthy on one side and a Queen's University medical student, Bill McKay, on the other. McKay was a robust and tireless player and a devastatingly effective tackler; McCarthy, a great opportunist who played off Kyle and had a liaison with the great out half that would prove extremely productive. Between McCarthy and McKay in the back row was the tall figure of Des O'Brien.

That victory in Paris was the preface to the most successful era in the history of Irish rugby.

England, at Twickenham, offered the next challenge and Ireland surmounted it by the narrowest of margins, 11-10, with Hugh De Lacey now Kyle's scrum half partner. Ireland scored three tries in the win at Twickenham.

Scotland came to Lansdowne Road with no fewer than three men who had played international rugby before the war. They proved no match for Ireland, however, who won readily enough after a very hesitant start. That victory meant that, irrespective of how matters went against Wales, to be encountered in Belfast, Ireland won the championship. But the Triple Crown was the objective; not since the closing years of the Victorian era, 1899, had Ireland won the great prize and few who travelled to Belfast on March 13th, 1948, had been in the crowd when Ireland won in Cardiff in 1899.

Ravenhill, Belfast, was packed to its 30,000 capacity and most of them came in expectation of witnessing an historic Irish triumph. Had Ravenhill the capacity to accommodate another 100,000 there is no doubt it would still have been full.

No sporting event up to that date had held the Irish public captive to such a degree, and Karl Mullen, who led Ireland that afternoon, still has vivid memories of the feeling in the Irish team prior to the match.

'We were well aware of the tension and air of expectation in the crowd and indeed throughout the whole country,' says Mullen. 'I felt we could win and I think that was the general feeling among the players. There was, of course, the psychological factor of not having won the Triple Crown for almost half a century and that imposed its additional burden. But to counter that, we felt this was the golden chance and that it must not be missed.

'We discussed our tactics and analysis of the Welsh team brought forth the conclusion that they had some great players; mistakes must be cut to a minimum. Indeed I think the ability to remain free from error at the crucial moments was a notable

The team that won the fourth Triple Crown, March 1949. Back row (l. to r.): C. R. Graves (touch judge), M. Lane, T. Clifford, W. D. McKee, L. Griffin, D. J. O'Brien, J. E. Nelson, G. Norton, J. W. McKay, T. Pearce (referee). Front row (l. to r.): J. S. McCarthy, R. D. Agar, K. D. Mullen (capt.), G. P. S. Hogan (President I.R.F.U.), B. O'Hanlon, N. J. Henderson. In front: J. W. Kyle, E. Strathdee.

characteristic of the Irish side of that period. Then we had Kyle, in my view incomparable before and since.

'It was after we beat England at Twickenham that thoughts of the Triple Crown really began to fertilise. We decided to put our faith in our forwards and leave Kyle to play to our strength. We knew that we had to win most of the possession as the Welsh backs would surely capitalise on a high ratio of possession. They had magnificent backs in men like Haydn Tanner, Bleddyn Williams and Ken Jones.

'We got a reasonable start. Barney Mullan put a kick just over the Welsh fullback's shoulder and the ball rather fortunately trickled into touch near the Welsh line. Somehow, I felt then it was going to be our day.

'I know that many people think that we had just one back of quality, in Kyle, but I do not agree at all. Kyle was the genius and the inspiration, but in defensive terms I think our backs were first class and our centres that day, Paddy Reid and Des McKee, were brilliant in defence. We had scoring power too on the wings.'

Well, Karl Mullen's reflections apart, Ireland took the lead when Barney Mullan scored a try after Kyle had given the scoring pass. Bleddyn Williams, however, equalised for Wales to leave it at 3–3 when the interval arrived.

There was to follow 40 minutes made memorable by their content as well as their climax.

Karl Mullen recalls the second period. 'We were having some trouble in the line out, particularly from Rhys Stephens, so Jimmy Nelson, that fine forward from Malone, was given the task of containing him, and how well he did it.

'We were the better side in the second half and the team showed tremendous application and discipline. It was J. C. Daly who was to emerge as the hero and he scored a try in the second half that separated victor from vanquished. In the closing stages, Kyle was magnificent as he sent the Welsh back time after time. The closing minutes were agonizingly long, but we survived'.

Karl Mullen remembers that, when the final whistle went, he was conscious of the crowd coming onto the field in waves. 'Yet it was hard to take in the fact that we had, after so long, won the Triple Crown; and that we had won the championship and the Grand Slam for good measure.'

That Grand Slam is, in fact, the only time Ireland has achieved the feat. The crowd went wild and Daly's jersey was torn from his back by souvenir hunters. Daly, who early in the season looked as if he would have to stop playing rugby because of a troublesome back injury, had been a stalwart in the front row, but sadly it was to be his last game for Ireland. It was no bad way to end. He turned professional and went on to fashion a distinguished career in the paid ranks.

Nine of the team that played in Belfast had played in all four matches, and so are unique in the annals of Irish rugby as the only men to figure in every match of an Irish Grand Slam. They deserve mention individually. They are Bertie O'Hanlon, Des McKee, Barney Mullan, Jack Kyle, A. A. McConnell, Colm Callan, Karl Mullen, Jim McCarthy, and Bill McKay. Three more played in the three Triple Crown games, Jimmy Nelson, Des O'Brien and J. C. Daly. Dudley Higgins played against France, Scotland and Wales, but was injured for the game against England and replaced by Jack Mattsson. Paddy Reid played against France, England and Wales; Hugh De Lacey against England and Scotland, but replaced at scrum half for the final game by Ernie Strathdee, who had played against France and was then dropped before being recalled for the Triple Crown decider. He was Kyle's partner at Queen's University and a durable player he was. Mick O'Flanagan, a brother of Kevin's and like Kevin a soccer international as well, played one game against Scotland; Ernie Keeffe, a second row from the Sunday's Well club in Cork, played in one game, as did Bob Agar and Jim Corcoran.

Naturally, the Grand Slam triumph gave a tremendous boost to the game in Ireland and, in the wake of such success, with most of the side again available, it was considered that Ireland could repeat their success in the 1949 campaign. Two of the men who were in the side in Belfast, Reid and Daly, had turned professional and joined the Huddersfield club.

When Ireland opened the 1949 campaign against France in Dublin, the Irish were warm favourites. It is a role in which Ireland have often been unhappy and one they have regularly failed to justify. This was no exception and, when France won, it was a considerable anticlimax and great disappointment.

Four new caps came into the side, one of them fullback George Norton was to leave a profound impact at a later stage. At prop, Daly was replaced by Tom Clifford from Limerick. Tom Cullen, a student at University College Dublin, was at scrum half and the old problem position in the centre was filled by Tom Gavin, from the London Irish club. Gavin came in against an unlikely background, but he is unique in the history of the game, for he was then and still is a Roman Catholic priest. Some men later to aspire to that noble calling played for Ireland, but no one other than Gavin has actually played rugby for Ireland after ordination.

France won 16–9 and their win owed nothing to good fortune. Norton kicked three penalty goals for Ireland, the opening shots, as it were, in what was to be a very fruitful career. A decision taken by the International Board had reduced the dropped goal from four to three points now, a circumstance that in fact meant France won by two points fewer than would have been the case 12 months earlier, as they scored two dropped goals in that fine win.

Kyle was again paired with Strathdee when the team to meet England was named. O'Hanlon was on one wing and Mick Lane on the other. He had failed to win a place the previous year after making his debut in 1947. Ireland beat England 14–5, but aspects of their play were singularly unimpressive. However the forwards had rekindled their old fire, and Mullen was still the master craftsman as hooker.

As was the case the previous year, the Ireland selectors did not hesitate to change a winning side if they felt such remedial action was necessary, and two of the pack, Callan and McConnell, were dropped for the visit to Murrayfield; as was Gavin, who was replaced by a young Queen's University student, Noel Henderson. For Henderson, this was the start of

what was to be a magnificent career, extending over a decade and embracing a Lions tour.

Bob Agar, a man of great experience, took over from Callan, and Les Griffin of Wanderers replaced McConnell.

Ireland's visit to Murrayfield did not represent an easy assignment, especially as Scotland too had reason to entertain championship hopes, following wins over France and Wales.

The great understanding between Kyle and McCarthy was demonstrated most effectively, however, and McCarthy scored two tries. Yet again Norton kicked the goals and the Scots were comprehensively beaten. So another Triple Crown beckoned and yet again Swansea was the venue. Could Ireland at last lay the Swansea bogey? They took an unchanged side to attempt the task of winning the crown and championship for the second successive year, a feat never previously attained by the Irish. They also took as many Irish followers as could get tickets for the encounter.

The Welsh had not had a very impressive championship, with their performances varying between the indifferent and the effective, but they had great experience and skill in their side and they were of course playing on home soil. They brought in the experienced Billy Cleaver for Glyn Davies at outside half.

The Ireland team that won the International Championship in 1951, the third triumph in the series in four years.

Once more the forwards did what was required of them. Kyle was brilliant and his partnership with McCarthy was to prove the match-winning factor. The game produced just one try and it was Kyle who fashioned it in the first half with a kick to the Welsh line, while the ever vigilant McCarthy was on hand to dive over the Welsh line and get the golden score. Norton converted.

Wales, as is their wont, did not die easily, but Ireland contained every assault and were full value for their win. So the Triple Crown and Championship had been claimed yet again, the Swansea bogey broken.

The Irish score had been the reward for enterprise and good timing, like so many scores achieved by Ireland in that period. In those days, there was no such terminology in the game as 'second phase attack', 'good ball and bad ball', 'screening'. Yet Ireland did play what might now be termed second phase attack and McCarthy was central figure in their strategy. In Kyle, they had just about the ideal man to play to the strength of the team and to conceal their weaknesses. His cover tackling was seldom less than brilliant, his perception acute, his footballing ability of the highest possible order. Kyle had great hands, a good turn of speed and the ability to make the break at just the right time. He was, without question, the outstanding back of that era, a fact recognised throughout the rugby world; and he was to captivate that most discerning of crowds, the New Zealanders, shortly after helping Ireland to those unprecedented heights of glory.

At that time, there were many outstanding players from overseas in British teams, and England and Scotland in particular were not averse to using their services. It caused some controversy prior to the 1950 campaign. The qualification laws were loose in the extreme, and in fact the playing of men from the dominions was not in any way illegal. The Irish, however, were rather more rigid. It was Irish birth or at least one Irish parent before a player was given consideration.

There was to be no hat-trick of Triple Crowns for Ireland, for next season it was the Welsh who captured the honours and the limelight.

There were a few changes on the Irish side which, in 1950, won one and drew one of the four matches. Luck was not smiling on Ireland that season. Against England, for instance, Ireland lost Des McKee and played with 14 men for the entire second half.

In the summer of 1950, the Lions went to New Zealand and Australia, the first touring side to leave the islands since the pre-war days. Ireland's great strength and level of achievement was reflected in the side which was led by Karl Mullen—who else after the splendid nature of his leadership with Ireland? Eight Irishmen accompanied him.

It was sea travel in those far-off days and apparently, the early stages of the journey were hard going. On the field, too, as one expected, it was rough and tough. New Zealand won the test series 3–0 with one drawn, and it was not an especially happy tour for Mullen who missed the third and fourth tests due to injury. George Norton broke an arm, thus depriving the Lions of a most accomplished full back and of equal importance, an ace goal kicker.

Mullen was ready for the Irish challenge in the 1951 campaign, and there were hopes that the Championship and Triple Crown might be regained. One ambition was realised, the second frustrated in agonizing fashion.

A new man was now at scrum half, John O'Meara, from Cork, and he was to hold down the berth for several seasons and prove Kyle's most regular partner. It was a great tribute to Kyle that he managed to maintain his excellence, despite the fact that his partners were so often changed.

It was something that did not worry Kyle and now in retrospect, he is quick to pay his tributes to those who served him. In all, no fewer than eight scrum halves played for Ireland with Kyle. Kyle believes the leadership of Mullen and the tremendous character in the side were essential elements.

Ireland won a narrow victory over France in the initial game of the 1951 series and then beat England in Dublin, by a penalty goal to nil. It was an undistinguished game, the one goal being kicked by Des McKibbin whose brother Harry had been a pre-war international. Indeed the number of brothers and fathers and sons who have played for Ireland has been truly remarkable, underlining the strong family traditions of the game in this country.

Against Scotland in Edinburgh, fortune dealt a fickle hand when Norton was injured early on and the team had to be rearranged. Harry Millar, of Queen's University, went from wing to fullback and Bill McKay from wing forward to the wing. The seven Irish forwards did a tremendous job, and once again Kyle was masterly. Ireland won, gaining yet another chance of the Crown, Championship and Grand Slam.

Ireland travelled to Cardiff on March 10th, but did so without Norton who was destined not to play again following that injury at Murrayfield. He had served the cause nobly. Many of the old stalwarts of the 1949 side had now gone, but a hard core remained, for the entire back row, Mullen and Kyle were all on hand. As events transpired Norton's absence was never more sorely missed, for kicking deficiencies cost Ireland the match.

Kyle scored a great try for Ireland and it was not converted, nor was there a single successful kick at goal by the Irish that whole afternoon, the game being drawn 3–3. It gave Ireland the Championship, but not the Triple Crown. The golden era was over.

John O'Meara, the Ireland scrum half, throws out a long pass to Jack Kyle in the 1951 International Championship match against England in Dublin. O'Meara, capped twenty-two times, was one of eight scrum halves to play for Ireland with Kyle.

THE FIFTIES

WHEN IRELAND won the International Championship in 1951, there was sufficient skill and experience still on hand to suggest that another title or two could be gathered by the Irish, even if many of the great Triple Crown side were now growing old together. The incomparable Kyle was still a young man and Jim McCarthy, his great ally in the tactical ploys of the golden era, still had much to give. Karl Mullen's medical duties were, however, imposing their own demands and an injury also restricted his activity.

Yet while there were some great victories, notable feats and significant events during the fifties, in terms of the Triple Crown and the Championship there was no really worthwhile challenge.

In every era Ireland has produced great players, and however unproductive the championship endeavour, the side maintained its tradition of sending out players of world class.

In the summer of 1952, there was an historic occasion when Ireland sent a team to Argentina and Chile under the management of Sarsfield Hogan. Mr. Hogan, president of the I.R.F.U. when Ireland won the Triple Crown in 1949, had given magnificent service to the game on the administrative side. As a player for University College, Dublin, and part of a great Lansdowne team of the late twenties, he had just missed an international cap. In the corridors of power, he reached the summit, with a world-wide reputation for his astuteness as a member of the International Board. That he should have been the choice as manager of the touring side in Argentina, was absolutely appropriate.

The Irish were unable to take anything like a full strength side to Argentina. Among those missing were Kyle and Mullen, and the side was captained by Des O'Brien. In all Ireland played nine matches, won six, drew two and lost one. They captured the two-match test series, by winning the second test 6–0 after a 3–3 draw in the first.

Among those who made the journey was an outside half from the Instonians club in Belfast, John Hewitt. This young man was a player of immense skill, but found himself in direct opposition to Kyle for the outside half position on the national side. There was considerable controversy at the time about using Hewitt's talents in other positions and that debate would be re-opened at a much later date when Ireland was again blessed with two outside halves of world repute—but here I anticipate.

As circumstances worked out, however, Hewitt gained but four caps, a very meagre return for so fine a talent.

By going to Argentina, Ireland followed a path England had already trodden, more than 50 years after an Ireland side had toured Canada in 1899.

Just before the visit to Argentina, it looked for a while as if the tour would be called off, owing to the death of Eva Peron, a national heroine in Argentina and the wife of the president. But the tour went ahead and was a great success, although it did not herald a fertile period for the Irish on the home front.

By 1953, Mullen and O'Brien (who had succeeded Mullen as captain for the 1952 championship series) were gone. Ireland defeated France in 1952 in Paris, and 20 long years would pass before they were to achieve that distinction again.

If proof were needed that Ireland no longer had the ability to win crowns and championships, it came at Lansdowne Road in March 1952, when Wales overwhelmed the Irish by 14–3. Cliff Morgan, who had emerged as an outside half in the very best Welsh tradition, certainly stamped his skills across the scene that afternoon. The match was touched with some sadness for Ireland as it was to be Karl Mullen's last appearance in the green jersey in which he had performed with such skill, dedication and success.

The game against England that season, postponed due to the death of King George VI, took place at the end of March, and Mullen was not in the team.

Then came the tour to Argentina, and that was to be the end of O'Brien's tenure on the national side.

Kyle was now Ireland's captain for the 1953 series, but he did not have the strength in depth at his side to meet the demands. There was a notable victory over Scotland at Murrayfield that season, with Ireland winning 26–8, while a young wing from the U.C.D. club, Seamus Byrne, scored three tries in the match to equal the record try-scoring achievements by an Irishman in an international.

The fourth All Blacks came in the autumn of 1953 and beat Ireland. Once more Munster gave the tourists a tremendous match, but failed in their quest to become the first Irish side to beat the All Blacks, the visitors getting a try in the last minute to save the day and their precious record. Munster would have another day.

In 1954, when Ireland met England at Twickenham, an Ireland side took the field without Kyle for the first time in the post war era. Kyle had to withdraw because of injury and so Hewitt at last got his cap.

There was no glory on hand during the next few years. McCarthy ended his career in 1955, but that season a young threequarter emerged on the scene from the Old Belvedere club, one Tony O'Reilly. O'Reilly won international recognition after a handful of senior games with his club. His red hair and very big build made him easily recognisable and his powerful stride made him very hard to stop when he decided to have a go for the line. O'Reilly was to have a long career, but it was in the Lions jersey rather than the Irish that he really made a profound impact.

J. W. Kyle scoring against France at Belfast in 1953—one of his greatest tries.

He was chosen for the Lions team to tour South Africa in 1955, when once more the choice of captain went to an Irishman, second row Robin Thompson who had led Ireland in three of the championship matches in 1955. The manager of the Lions was also an Irishman, Jack Siggins. In his time he had been a good forward for Ireland and was a perceptive administrator. Ireland had five players in the touring party.

The Lions did extremely well drawing the test series. O'Reilly scored 16 tries in South Africa, a then record number, and he ended the tour as top scorer. His colleagues from Ireland on the touring side were Tom Reid, Robin Roe, now established as Ireland's hooker in succession to Mullen, Thompson, and Cecil Pedlow, a very good centre from Belfast.

Kyle played his last game for Ireland against Scotland in Dublin in 1958, going out on a winning streak as Ireland won 12-6. It was the second honour he had gathered before the last accolade, for he was in the Ireland side that beat Australia at Lansdowne Road, a few weeks before that victory over Scotland. Ireland beat Australia 9-6 and so recorded the first victory over a major touring side. The team was captained by another survivor from the golden era, Noel Henderson, still giving marvellous service in the green jersey. John O'Meara had been recalled for the game, so no fewer than three of the men who

In January 1958, Ireland beat a touring team for the first time when Australia lost at Lansdowne Road. Here Noel Henderson, a member of the Ireland side that won the Triple Crown in 1949, shows that his powers did not diminish in ten seasons of international rugby as he scores the winning try for Ireland.

had helped win the championship in 1951 were on hand when Ireland scored their historic win over the Wallabies.

The team that beat Australia also saw the debut in international rugby of three men who would later captain Ireland, and one who was destined to lead the Lions. The last of these, Ronnie Dawson, is now one of the leading figures in the game's administration as an Irish representative on the International Board. Quite apart from his distinguished playing career, Dawson was to leave a tremendous impact on the scene as an innovator and advocate of proper coaching and preparation for international sides.

That afternoon against Australia, he marked his debut by scoring a try. It was Henderson, however, who won the match for Ireland by scoring the try that created the decisive margin between the sides.

In addition to Dawson, the two great forwards Noel Murphy and Bill Mulcahy made their debuts against Australia, and both went on to play for the Lions and captain Ireland. Murphy came from a family whose roots were deeply embedded in the game. His father, Noel senior, had been a very good Irish forward in the thirties, while the family connection with the Constitution club in Cork had been established from its foundation. Murphy won 41 caps as a flank forward and is acknowledged as among the best to have played in that position in the post war era.

Mulcahy, a Munsterman, assumed leadership of Ireland in 1962, by which time Dawson had already been Ireland's regular captain and also led the Lions to New Zealand in 1959.

When Kyle retired, the choice of successor fell on Mick English who came from the same club in

Limerick as Mulcahy, Bohemians. As events turned out, however, both were to play much of their club rugby in Dublin, Mulcahy with the University College Dublin and Bective Rangers clubs and English with the great Lansdowne club.

When the fifties came to a close, the contrast for Ireland was sharp between the glorious manner in which the decade had opened and the rather erratic performances and form of the side in 1959.

Dawson was now captain and showed a keen tactical brain and ready appreciation of the strengths and weaknesses at his command.

The Irish pack was strong with Dawson propped

Tony O'Reilly scoring the last of his record thirty-eight tries for the Lions in the final test in 1959 against New Zealand during the Lions' 9–6 win. His try-scoring achievements still stand as records in both South Africa and New Zealand.

by two men of immense strength in Syd Millar and Gordon Wood, both later to be honoured by the Lions. Mulcahy had Gerry Culliton as his second row partner and both had long and distinguished careers in the green jersey. Culliton, from Wanderers, was also very versatile, playing for Ireland in three different forward positions and serving in all with great diligence and effect.

Murphy had now established himself in the back row and Ronnie Kavanagh was still around, while a very good forward from Connacht, Tony O'Sullivan, had also emerged from an excellent side of the late fifties. For long the cinderella province in Irish rugby, Connacht was now becoming a force to be reckoned with, a tribute to much dedicated work in an area predominantly devoted to the Gaelic football and hurling codes. Men such as Henry Anderson, Henry Blake, Jim Keane and Chris

Crowley had rendered magnificent service to the game in Connacht and now that was paying off, although there would be lean times again for the men from the far west of Ireland.

When Ireland opened their challenge in 1959, Henderson was still around and played at full back. O'Reilly was in the centre and another Connacht man, John Dooley, his partner. An exciting young prospect had emerged on the wing in Nial Brophy, a product of Ireland's greatest rugby school, Blackrock College. Pedlow occupied the other wing and English was partnered at half back by Andy Mulligan, from Cambridge University, a man of some wit as well as wisdom.

There was considerable optimism about the prospects at the outset of the season, but it was ill founded. England, who with Wales had been the dominant force in the fifties, beat Ireland 3-0 at Lansdowne Road, and that was the end of Triple Crown hopes. David Hewitt, an exciting young centre who had come into the side in the aftermath of the golden era and was a member of a great Belfast rugby family, was recalled for the game against Scotland at Murrayfield, which Ireland won. The Scottish ground was a very fertile plain indeed for the Irish at this period.

John Hewitt got an unexpected call to the colours for the game in Cardiff against Wales when English was ill, but despite this Wales won the match.

Now the final game of the fifties was set for Lansdowne Road on April 18th 1959, with France the opposition. It was an historic occasion, for France had won the championship with that one game still to play. It was the first time in history that the French had won the title and they came to Lansdowne Road generally expected to win and add lustre to their great season.

Yet again, the Irish proved to be gloriously unpredictable. France had beaten Scotland and Wales and drawn with England and, such had been the pattern of results, that five points had already assured the French of the title under the inspiring leadership of Lucian Mias.

Dawson led Ireland splendidly and got a great response from his forwards. The backs too played extremely well with English restored at out half and a new and exciting young teenager, Kevin Flynn, from Wanderers, playing in the centre. Ireland built a 6-0 interval lead and the French just could not contain the rampant men in green. Henderson was at fullback for his last and 38th cap. It was a splendid end to a notable career.

So the fifties ended in a great and unexpected win. There had been a few other memorable victories against the general expectation—against Wales in 1956 for instance—but no crown and no title.

The tremendous enthusiasm and interest generated by the deeds of Karl Mullen and his men had a very good effect generally on the scene in Ireland. The game was more popular than at any time in history, and more people were playing and watching it. The growth was not as spectacular as was later to be the case when television did a great promotion job for the game, but rugby in Ireland, at the end of the fifties, was thriving.

To meet the increased demand for stand tickets for the internationals, there was major reconstruction of the west stand at Lansdowne Road that increased the capacity of the ground to over 50,000. A four-countries match was played to mark its official opening. Rupert Jeffares, the first paid secretary of the I.R.F.U., had retired by now and been succeeded by his son Billy. Harry Thrift, player and legislator extraordinary, announced in 1956 that he was retiring as honorary secretary of the International Board and another Irishman, Eddie Kirwan, was elected to take his place. It was on to the sixties with renewed hope and no little element of confidence.

THE REVOLUTIONARY SIXTIES

WHEN future generations go down the avenues of historical investigation in search of landmarks in the development and evolution of the game, I feel sure many will conclude that the decade of the 1960s must rank as the most significant period of all. There had been a few other very important times of development, yet none, perhaps, to quite match the sixties.

In the early days of international rugby, there were men ready to work to make the game more appealing to play and more attractive to watch. To this end the number of players on each side had been reduced to 15 and Ireland, as it happened, had been involved in the first 15-a-side international. The closing years of the 19th century and the early years of the 20th, saw back play come more into its own, with the Welsh having a particularly important influence. Then in the twenties and thirties, forward play became more sophisticated. After the resumption of internationals in 1947, the French influence was brought to bear with great ball-carrying forwards, and elaborate line-out strategy.

The sixties saw the advent of the television set in almost every sitting-room; it was the era when modern travel facilities became so good that man could cross the world in under 24 hours. It was the period when a great deal of thought went into strategy, when films of the opposition were carefully studied, and when there was an unprecedented quest for physical fitness so that sides could play to their maximum ability and counter opposition strengths. By the close of the decade, replacements were being allowed in international matches and that, in some respects, was remarkable, for such a move had been regularly resisted by the more conservative of the rugby legislators, the argument being that it might be abused. The argument was not sustained, however, and rugby decided late in the decade to allow replacements in international rugby; that decision was later extended to embrace the game at club level.

Irish rugby did not, I believe, lose its essential character in the midst of all the changes, but it did go through a very difficult period, notably early in the decade when success on the international field was very meagre and defeat a much more frequent visitor than victory.

Yet in the manner that these things sometimes happen, some players were to come on the scene in the Ireland jersey whose feats would be indelibly etched into the game's history. When Ireland went to Twickenham in 1960, they included a full back from University College Cork, Tom Kiernan. His advent on the scene did not coincide with victory and his early games in the green jersey saw little tangible reward. Perhaps the fluid nature of the position is best summed up by the fact that, when Ireland went to Twickenham in 1962, they included no fewer than nine new caps as the selectors sought remedial action in alteration. The new formula was not successful, however; England won readily by 16-0 and some of those who wore the Ireland jersey that afternoon would not do so again. But there were two debutants in the side that afternoon who would be around for quite some time and who would, before they left the international scene, share in a number of historic achievements. The players were both forwards, one a prop, Ray McLoughlin, the other a second row, Willie John McBride.

When Jack Kyle retired from the scene in 1958, he did so with 46 caps, an all time record. That record was to be eclipsed by not just one of the men of the sixties, but by three, McBride, Kiernan and Michael Gibson, who had not yet arrived in 1962, but whose prowess was being sharpened in the colours of the Wanderers club in Dublin and then the Cambridge University team.

Gibson first attracted what one might term

34

The Ireland team that included nine new caps and played England at Twickenham in 1962. Though Ireland lost 16–0 in this game, two of the newcomers, Ray McLoughlin and Willie John McBride, went on to captain Ireland, and McBride became the world's most capped forward with sixty-three appearances for Ireland and a record seventeen tests for the Lions. McBride is sixth from the left in the back row and McLoughlin second from the left in the front row.

international attention when he played magnificently in the Cambridge side that won the 1963 Varsity match. Within a few weeks of his five-star performance in that game, he was named in the Ireland side to meet England at Twickenham, and that afternoon he devastated England from the outside half position as Ireland won a famous victory. By now, the faltering steps so apparent early in the decade were changing to more decisive leaps forward and there was tremendous hope and confidence that Ireland would revive old glories in 1964. However, in keeping with their frustrating facility for the unexpected, they lost to Scotland in Dublin; and so another dream died.

Ireland had gone to South Africa in the summer of 1961 under the leadership of Ronnie Dawson, a mission not blessed with success. The Springboks scored a ready test win, but the experience was valuable and some of it was now coming to Ireland's aid.

The Lions went to South Africa in 1962 and Ireland managed to get six players in the side, Kiernan, Brophy, David Hewitt, Syd Millar, Bill Mulcahy and Willie John McBride, then a raw youngster from Ballymena. He would return to South Africa many years later to climb to unprecedented heights of glory, but no such pleasures were on hand for the 1962 Lions.

For Ireland the progress was steady rather than in any way spectacular as the sixties entered mid stream, but immediately there was a move that was to prove highly significant, and at the centre of it was Ray McLoughlin.

It was decided that McLoughlin would be captain of the Ireland side. A native of Ballinasloe in County Galway, and a member of the Connacht side, he played his rugby in University College, Dublin, before studies took him to Gosforth in the north of England.

McLoughlin brought to that task a dedication that had as its aim the pursuit of excellence.

Ronnie Dawson, during his term of captaincy of the national side, tightened things considerably by the thoroughness of his preparation, then very much a matter for the captain; the day of the coach had not yet arrived.

McLoughlin's ideas were an extension of Dawson's thoroughness. McLoughlin was intense, thoughtful to the last degree, meticulous in his own personal preparation and quest for physical fitness, and he imposed equal demands on those at his side. He was, unquestionably, marginally ahead of his time, yet his contribution can never be underestimated. Some

might say of him that he was not flexible enough in tactical approach, yet he brought a new concept to his task and things were never quite the same again.

Some of the establishment did not like the new order. Maybe his greatest fault was that he attempted to do too much too quickly. Yet his approach was to be emulated within a very short time. His period as captain of Ireland did not last long, nor was it blessed with success, if success be judged by Triple Crowns and Championships. The significance of his reign should not, nonetheless be under-valued for all that. McLoughlin was a visionary and, like many in that category before him, he did not reap the benefits of his thought and his labours.

McLoughlin led an Irish side to a Triple Crown decider at the Arms Park in 1965, but like many another side of the past, it faltered at the final hurdle on Welsh soil.

The atmosphere at the Arms Park was intense that afternoon, and by now, of course, television had entered the scene with all the matches being televised, a circumstance that enabled thousands of Irish supporters to see the match on their screens when they could not get tickets to see it 'live'.

They saw the tension get to Kiernan, who missed an early penalty chance; it was that kind of afternoon for the Irish. It was a very disappointing encounter, won deservedly by Wales, for whom Terry Price was a major contributor, sealing the win for his side in the closing stages.

So McLoughlin had failed to win the Triple Crown with a very good side that saw two men in particular emerge as international players of great substance. Ken Kennedy had won the hooking berth and he was to stay around for a decade and win a world record 45 caps in the position. Another who came on the scene at that time was flanker Mick Doyle, who had been a team-mate of Gibson's at Cambridge University. Both would figure in historic achievements within a short space of time.

The afternoon of the 10th April 1965 is a very significant date in the annals of Irish rugby, for that day Ireland beat the Springboks for the first time in history and McLoughlin was the man who led Ireland to victory.

South Africa had come on a five match tour to Ireland and Scotland. This was the era when the short tour came into its own, but short tours can be hazardous missions as even the great Springboks found to their cost. On a brief stay a touring team does not get the chance to acclimatise, build up teamwork and confidence.

The Springboks had opened their tour with a

lucky draw against a Combined Provinces side in Belfast and seemed in no imminent danger on a visit to Thomond Park, the famous ground in Limerick where the opposition was to be provided by the Combined Universities. With the international against Ireland only a few days away, the Universities could not select players who had been named for Ireland, this limiting their options to a great degree.

The Universities were denied the services of McLoughlin, Kiernan, wing Pat McGrath, Kennedy, Mulcahy and scrum half Roger Young, a dental student from Queen's University, Belfast, who now emerged on the national side after a brief club apprenticeship. The Universities side was led by Jerry Walsh, a magnificent defensive centre, whose tackling was rated to be the best in the game at that period.

The Universities led all the way in a memorable match and eventually held on for a 12-10 victory, thus becoming the first Irish side to beat the Springboks. That the win was achieved on Limerick soil was very appropriate, as this great rugby city, where the game is the preserve not of a certain level of society but of all, more than any deserved to be the venue for such a success. It was great too that the first defeat of the Springboks should come on Munster soil, for the province had been unlucky so many times against touring teams.

The win by the Universities was a major boost to Ireland, but the Springboks captain, Avril Malan, was in no mood to compromise. At the after match dinner, he told the gathering that, 'the Springboks had very little practice at losing'. Within a few days, they were to get another object lesson.

The game at Lansdowne Road was played in a blustery wind and intermittent showers, even though it was the middle of April. Ireland took an early lead with an initiative by Young paving the way for a try by McGrath. The Springboks equalised with a penalty goal. A 3-3 interval scoreline was scant reward for a lot of Springboks pressure, but Ireland held firm.

Now Ireland had the wind and the crowd behind them and looked set to take command, but it was the Springboks who scored when one of their centres, Mans, got in for a try. Kiernan, however, equalised that with a penalty. Then the crowd erupted into acclamation when Gibson scored a try, but to their dismay and that of the Irish players the try was disallowed for an infringement.

But there was a grand finale, and Kiernan provided it. He kicked a great penalty that held the crowd breathless while the ball sped on a low

trajectory to its objective.

Ireland won, and the Springboks' invincibility on Irish soil had been well and truly shattered, not once but twice in the space of four days.

By the following season, McLoughlin had surrendered the leadership of the side. After leading the team for three matches, he lost the captaincy for the final game against Wales to Kiernan. To this day, there is an element of controversy surrounding the decision and a belief that it was motivated, not only by some officials who resented McLoughlin's power, but a few players too, whose mutterings suggested they were not happy. Ironically, one man who did not offer any criticism was the man who succeeded him, Tom Kiernan.

Kiernan led the side in the final match of the 1966 campaign, but it was Noel Murphy who was in command the following season.

By this time, Bill Mulcahy had gone and a young medical student from Galway, Mick Molloy, had arrived in the second row to partner McBride, who had missed just one game since his debut. McBride was dropped for the match against Wales in 1964 and replaced by Mick Leahy, from Cork. Leahy won one cap only, but can claim one very important distinction: he was the only man ever to gain preference over McBride for an Irish jersey.

The decision of the Ireland selectors to take the captaincy from McLoughlin for the final game of the 1966 series, almost certainly cost him the distinction of leading the Lions to Australia and New Zealand in 1966 when the choice as leader fell to Mike Campbell-Lamerton of Scotland. Des O'Brien, the man who had been centre stage in the Triple Crown years, was made manager. Frankly, in retrospect, there is no doubt they did not make a very potent combination. That tour was something of a disaster.

When the fifth Wallabies came to Britain and Ireland in the autumn of 1966, it was Noel Murphy who led the side to victory, Ireland's second win over the Wallabies. A feature of this achievement was that Mike Gibson dropped two goals in a comprehensive success, while Alan Duggan, a wing from Lansdowne who had been capped a few years previously, was back on the scene and scored a try that afternoon. He was later to get 10 more in a fine international career.

Four days after the game in Dublin, Australia travelled to Musgrave Park, Cork, to face Munster and, as the southern province had threatened so often, they at last succeeded in beating the Wallabies (11-8, with Kiernan getting eight points). John Moroney, of London Irish, got a try. That Munster side included Noel Murphy, but it was Kiernan who captained Munster to historic victory, the first by an Irish provincial team over a major touring side. There would be a greater day in the years ahead for the men of Munster and the scalp would be even more distinguished.

Ireland did not manage to mount a challenge for the Triple Crown and championship during 1967, but the side was a good one and played tremendously well in beating Wales at Cardiff, with Duggan getting a try, the only score of the game. Scotland had been beaten at Murrayfield with Murphy getting a try and his cousin Kiernan the conversion. France came to Dublin for the final match of the season and won readily 11-6.

Murphy, meanwhile, had been named as captain for Ireland's first tour to Australia in the summer of 1967, but had to withdraw for business reasons. Kiernan took over the leadership, and that decision was to have a very significant bearing on future events, leading to a record tenure of office as Ireland's leader.

The Irish party was chosen with one of the great players of the past, Eugene Davy, as manager and Des McKibbin as his assistant. They left Dublin on April 22nd and glory was on the horizon.

The tour embraced six games, including one test, and the magnitude of the Irish task can be emphasised by the fact that no team from the Four Countries had ever won a test match in the southern hemisphere. That was finally rectified on May 13th in Sydney when Ireland scored a memorable success.

What made the victory all the more acceptable and surprising was that Ireland had lost the previous week on the same ground to New South Wales. In the international, the Irish played with tremendous character.

Ireland, too, had major injury problems which meant that they had to make and mend behind the scrum. Barry Bresnihan, a big and strong centre who had come onto the international scene in 1966, was injured, so Pat McGrath was moved from wing to centre and Nial Brophy, now in the veteran class, came onto the side at wing. The pack included one new cap, the big Highfield number eight, Terry Moore.

For Kiernan, the match was especially significant, as he won his 33rd cap and so equalled the world record in the position held by W. J. Bancroft of Wales.

Jerry Walsh gave Ireland the lead with a try after good work by the scrum half Brendan Sherry, from Terenure College Club. Kiernan converted. Then just after half time, Kiernan dropped a goal to give

Ireland an 8-0 lead. Australia cut the deficit with five points, but McGrath soon got another try for Ireland to give his side an 11-5 lead.

But Ireland had laboured for much of the game under the handicap of a severe injury to Sherry, who of course could not be replaced in those days. The medical skills of the Ireland team doctor Jamesy Maher kept Sherry on the field.

So Ireland, the great unpredictables, had done it again.

There are many who believe that the All Blacks side that came to Britain in the autumn of 1967 was the greatest of all touring sides to visit the British shores. Unfortunately the Irish public did not see the team. An outbreak of foot and mouth disease in Britain meant that the Irish government, mindful of the necessity for taking every possible precaution against its spread to Ireland, were relieved when the game due for Dublin in December 1967 was cancelled. It was a great disappointment for the Irish and the All Blacks, but an eminently sensible decision.

Ireland thus started the 1968 campaign with some disadvantage as, while they had not played an international, the other countries had. The All Blacks game against Scotland was marked by the dismissal from the field of the great All Blacks forward Colin Meads. He was sent off by the referee, Dublin schoolteacher Kevin Kelleher. It was the first time since the mid twenties that a man had been dismissed in an international and caused major controversy. Kelleher was one of many great Irish referees and a testimony to his ability is the fact that he shares with the Welshman Gwyn Walters the distinction of having taken charge of no fewer then 21 matches, a world record.

Ireland made the usual unproductive trip to Paris at the start of the 1968 campaign; it was now 16 years since they had last won in the French capital. At Twickenham, Ireland drew 9-9 with England, and England got that draw thanks to their full back, Bob Hiller, who kicked a last minute penalty from the touchline. Hiller was to prove a real scourge to the Irish in the years immediately ahead.

Ireland beat Scotland, and then it was Wales in Dublin. Wales, at this stage, were assembling an array of talent later to leave a profound impact on the scene. Gareth Edwards was at scrum half, Barry John his partner. Wales had decided that it was now necessary to have a coach for their national side. All other countries would soon follow suit, but at the time, not everyone agreed with the idea.

Ireland gave the Welsh a torrid afternoon in 1968,

The Doyle brothers, Mick (left) and Tom (right) close in on Welsh scrum half Gareth Edwards during the match between Ireland and Wales at Lansdowne Road in 1968. The Doyles, from Kerry, are one of forty-six sets of brothers who have played for Ireland, a remarkable number and one that emphasises the strong family traditions of Irish rugby.

and when they led 6–3 well into the second period, it seemed that victory was assured. There followed an incident that caused major controversy. Gareth Edwards took a drop at goal that went wide, but the referee M. H. Titcomb of England, deemed the kick good. The crowd behind the goal, who had a clear view of the kick, made their views known and the decision threatened to deprive Ireland of victory— 'another injustice to old Ireland', would be the cry. But it was not to be. Mick Doyle scored a try in the closing stages that gave Ireland a deserved win. Incidentally Doyle, a veterinary student from the predominantly Gaelic football region of Kerry, had his brother Tom in the side with him that afternoon.

So a win over Wales made a good end to the season, even if controversy was the keynote.

Meanwhile, the Lions were due to go to South Africa in the summer of 1968 and there was much debate about who would lead the side. The Welsh captain John Dawes was a leading contender, but that defeat in Dublin did not help his cause. In the end the choice fell on Kiernan and it was an Irishman, Ronnie Dawson, who was named as coach with England's David Brooks named as manager.

The Lions lost the test series, but did very well overall, winning 15 of their 20 matches. The Lions scored 38 points in the four-match test series and Kiernan accounted for 35 of them. The other three came from a try scored by Willie John McBride. But the Lions managed to draw just one test and lost the other three and, however well they did in the provincial games, it was the test series that really mattered.

The question of coaching was getting a great airing at this time and Dawson was at the forefront of the debate. When he came back from South Africa he spelled out loud and clear exactly what he thought was required. Dawson, who had captained and coached Lions sides, could draw on vast experience at first hand and felt that, unless, action were taken, the game in Britain and Ireland would fall even further behind the All Blacks and Springboks, the arch rivals. Not everyone in power wanted to hear or act on what he had to say, but it was pertinent and his voice was eventually heard.

It was at this time, too, that the replacement law came into being and Barry Bresnihan, the Ireland centre, became the first replacement in history when he came on during a game in the early stages of the Lions tour.

The 'Australian dispensation' was also brought into the laws, first on an experimental basis and then permanently. This decreed that a player could not kick directly to touch between the 25 yards lines. If he did so the touch was ordered from the place where the ball was kicked. The Australians themselves were the first to put the new law to the test when they met Ireland in Dublin in October 1968. Ireland won an undistinguished match 10-3 and it was not a good advertisement for the new laws.

If coaching as a general and necessary principle took some time to catch on in Ireland, the province of Leinster was ready to spread the gospel in this direction. As far back as 1964, the provincial branch instigated an annual course in the Butlin's Holiday camp at Mosney, County Meath, and the work done in this field by pioneers such as Judge Charles Conroy and Des Scaife was later to prove extremely beneficial.

But when the Irish set out on the campaign trail in 1969, the national team did not yet have a coach and team preparation was still the preserve of the captain, Tom Kiernan.

Ireland started well and beat France in Dublin. That win broke an 11-year sequence of defeats at the hands of the French. A notable absentee from the Irish side was Mike Gibson, who was recovering from a fractured cheek bone.

In Gibson's absence, the outside half berth was given to Barry McGann, a Munsterman who was playing with the Lansdowne club. His debut was memorable and of such proportions that when Gibson was fit, it was decided to move him to centre and retain McGann. The game against France also saw a record established. John Moroney, playing out of position on the wing (he was an outside half for his club London Irish), scored 14 points to set an individual record for an Irish player in an international.

The game was also the first occasion that Ireland used a replacement, the Terenure back row forward Mick Hipwell who came on for the injured Noel Murphy.

Ireland beat England 17-15 in a thrilling encounter in Dublin and even the dreaded Hiller could not foil Ireland, although he had a mighty good try. Again, Ireland used a replacement, Colin Grimshaw of Queen's University, coming on at scrum half for Roger Young.

Ireland had now won five matches in a row, and when Scotland was defeated at Murrayfield, the sequence became six, the longest winning run ever by an Ireland side. The win at Murrayfield also set up the Triple Crown and Grand Slam chance against Wales in Cardiff.

The pre-match publicity for the game was tremendous, and all sorts of theories and accusations got an airing. One was that Ireland had been violating the line out laws and getting away with it. Certainly there seems to have been a belief current in Wales that the Irish were going to carry some deadly and secret plan into battle, and this was the reputation that preceded Ireland to Wales. Ireland had to play without the assistance of number eight Ken Goodall, a forward from the City of Derry club, who had made a tremendous impact on the international scene. The choice fell to Hipwell to replace the Ulsterman.

The game against Wales was played on March 8th, before a crowd of only 25,000. This was due not to a lack of interest—on the contrary, the enthusiasm was intense—but to a major rebuilding project in

The Ireland team pictured before the controversial match against Wales at the Arms Park in 1969. Flanker Noel Murphy, second from the right in the back row, was punched in the early stages of the match. It was Murphy's last appearance for Ireland—he had won forty-one caps and was the world's most capped flanker until overtaken by Fergus Slattery.

progress at the Arms Park that reduced capacity to 25,000. Pleas to have the match played at another venue fell on deaf ears. The Welsh would not surrender home advantage, especially as Ireland was in pursuit of the Triple Crown. For the Welsh, it was only the second game of their programme, but vital for all that.

The Welsh had now assembled a team that was destined to win honours unprecedented in the game's history, and if on that March afternoon they did not reach their peak of brilliance, they nevertheless easily won in a match that did absolutely nothing to enhance the game and its ethos.

In the early stages of the match, an incident occurred that ruined the game. Brian Price, the vastly experienced Welsh forward, punched Noel Murphy in full view of the referee and most of the crowd, which included the Prince of Wales. Murphy fell to the ground, but the referee allowed Price to stay on the field.

Many and varied have been the explanations for Price's action, but it seems to have been a hasty and ill-conceived act perpetrated in the excitement of the moment. The game was held up after the incident and, for a time, it seemed as if it would have major repercussions. But play was resumed after the referee, Mr. McMahon of Scotland, had warned Price. It seemed a very inadequate punishment to fit the crime.

Wales won by the very convincing margin of 24–11 and so took a vital step towards winning the Triple Crown and Championship, twin ambitions that were subsequently realised.

It was in fact Murphy's last match and a very sad end to a distinguished career that earned him 41 caps and two Lions tours. So there was no dividend for Ireland in a season that had promised so much, and the sixties had come to an end. The turbulent sixties, some have called them, turbulence that found an echo at the Arms Park on March 8th.

DAWSON MAKES HIS POINT

THE STRENUOUS pleas of men such as Ronnie Dawson for proper preparation and coaching at last got a response when the I.R.F.U. decided in the autumn of 1969 to appoint a coach to the Irish side. The choice rightly fell on Dawson himself, easily the most experienced man on hand.

The first game under the new order was against South Africa in Dublin on January 10th, 1970. That Springboks side travelled around Britain and Ireland to a chorus of objections to their presence. They had a torrid time. Whatever the honest views held on the apartheid issue, some of the protests were far too vigorous in tone and in content. They seemed to echo the very intolerance that so many objected to in the South African way of life and the policy of the South African government.

The game against Ireland took place with the playing area well protected against possible incursion by the crowd. It all seemed rather unreal, and in fact the match was not a very memorable affair, ending in a draw with Ireland getting that equaliser through a late penalty from Kiernan. It was a reasonable enough first result for Ronnie Dawson.

Ronnie Dawson, Ireland's first national coach, 1970–72, was capped twenty-seven times for Ireland, captain of Ireland 1958–61 and captain of the Lions in New Zealand and Australia in 1959. He is now one of the game's leading legislators, being a member of the International Board, and was also coach to the Lions in South Africa in 1968.

Ken Goodall, extreme right, being congratulated by his team mate Alan Duggan and enthusiastic spectators after he scored a memorable try against Wales at Lansdowne Road in 1970.

Ireland that afternoon included a new cap at flank forward, Fergus Slattery, then a student at University College Dublin. He played with sufficient skill to suggest a long career, but no one in the crowd that afternoon could possibly have forecast just how long and distinguished that career would prove to be.

The great reserve of experience Dawson had at his command now needed to be supplemented with young players of skill, and Slattery was certainly in that category. The forward unit was now exceptionally strong, with vast experience in the front row where Kennedy was propped by Syd Millar and the ebullient Phil O'Callaghan of Dolphin, quick of tongue and strong of limb.

Millar had rather extraordinarily been banished to the wilderness for five years between 1963 and 1968, and yet on his return had been deemed good

enough to earn Lions selection. O'Callaghan had plenty of tough competition for his berth and had a long career of mixed fortune. McBride and Mick Molloy were in the second row and in the back row the number eight berth was held down by Ken Goodall, a man many considered to be the best in the position available to any country. He had immense promise that he was now beginning to realise. Ronnie Lamont was the other flanker and this great forward was extremely unlucky to suffer a bad arm injury that severely restricted his activities. He fought his way back to fitness, even though he did not have 100 per cent use of the arm.

The half backs were Young and McGann; Gibson was in the centre with Barry Bresnihan; Duggan and Bill Brown, of Malone, were on the wings and Kiernan was still at full back. It was a side that gave reason for optimism, but that optimism was crushed in Paris where yet again Ireland foundered.

Ireland's next assignment was against England at Twickenham and there were sensational developments on the eve of the match. Brown was forced to withdraw and, to the astonishment of the rugby world, the selectors sent for Tony O'Reilly, then a major figure in the business world and a man who had played just a handful of games that season. So O'Reilly was back on the international scene after seven years absence to win his 29th cap. His return was not a success, a circumstance that did not help the Irish selectors who came in for tremendous criticism as a result of the selection. Once more Ireland perished at Twickenham, and yet again it was Bob Hiller who applied the *coup de grâce*, dropping two magnificent goals to give England a 9-3 win. Not since Oliver Cromwell had an Englishman inflicted so much damage on the Irish.

A win over Scotland in Dublin brought a very welcome relief, and now the final assignment was against Wales at Lansdowne Road, a Welsh side in full cry for the Triple Crown and including J. P. R. Williams, John Dawes, Barry John, Gareth Edwards, and Mervyn Davies. They were the warmest of favourites to beat Ireland, but things turned out very differently as the Irish played magnificently to overwhelm the Welsh. It was sweet compensation for the previous year's *débacle*. Ireland won 14-0 as the Welsh crumpled before the challenge. The Irish forwards destroyed their opponents and Goodall in particular was brilliant, while behind, McGann played with masterly precision at out half; Kiernan at full back was at his best, and Goodall scored a try still remembered to this day. Alan Duggan also got a memorable try. It was a good preparation for Ireland's tour to Argentina later that summer.

The tour, Ireland's second to Argentina, began in August 1970, and the visit was to have consequences far removed from the rugby field. Ireland had to travel without Mike Gibson, Roger Young, Fergus Slattery and Ken Kennedy—some of their best players.

There were seven matches on the tour, of which Ireland won four and lost three, including the two tests. It was not a very satisfactory outcome. Some young players, who were then uncapped, made the journey and the experience they gained was later to prove invaluable. The U.C.D. wing Tom Grace and the St. Mary's College scrum half John Moloney were two of the most promising of the younger school on the tour. Paddy Madigan, a hooker from Old Belvedere who had been on the fringe of the Irish side, was also included in the touring party. It was some compensation for a fine player who had only failed to gain the ultimate distinction because of the level of competition, notably the expertise of Ken Kennedy.

Only one game was played outside Buenos Aires,

Roger Young, capped twenty-six times for Ireland between 1965 and 1971 as scrum half, in action against Wales at Lansdowne Road.

Alan Duggan, capped twenty-five times and Ireland's leading try scorer in international rugby, seen here scoring one of his memorable tries against Wales in 1970.

in Rosario, and the long stay in the Argentine capital was not ideal for any touring team. The refereeing was unsatisfactory, while in one match Phil O'Callaghan was sent off the field. It all added up to a rather indifferent tour. The journey home was to capture the headlines, however, in a way the on-field happenings had not.

The Irish party, en route for home, found themselves ordered off the aeroplane at Rio de Janeiro. The airline said that the party had been guilty of misconduct and that this was the reason for the decision to take them off the plane; that allegation has been categorically denied by everyone concerned. It appears that the airline had some other difficulty, such as overbooking, and that the removal of the Irish party solved its problems. The I.R.F.U. threatened to take legal action over the matter but in fact did not do so, a decision that did not satisfy many of the players who were on the plane. They felt they had been badly maligned and that the parent body had not done anything about it. The difficulties of international law, however, and the money involved, probably decided the I.R.F.U. against further action.

Kiernan was still the man at the helm when Ireland opened the 1971 championship campaign with a match against France in Dublin; he had now broken the 46-cap record of Jackie Kyle. The 1971 championship was not, however, to be distinguished by Kiernan's presence for very long. He broke a leg in that first match and was replaced by Barry O'Driscoll, a player who had long stood in the shadows of the great Corkman and now came to the centre of the stage in his own right.

It seemed unlikely that, at over 30, Kiernan would be seen in the Ireland jersey again, but this presumption proved incorrect. Ireland drew with France, and then England came to Lansdowne Road and once again that man Hiller fashioned an England victory. Would Ireland ever see the back of him?

Ireland as usual beat Scotland that year, but were comprehensively beaten by Wales who went on to Triple Crown glory yet again. Not this time the great flair and fire that had characterised Ireland's win the previous year.

A feature of the Ireland side of 1971 was that it saw the return to the international scene of Ray McLoughlin, after five years' absence. On the other side in the front row was Sean Lynch, from the St. Mary's College Club in Dublin, while at number eight was Denis Hickie, also from St. Mary's College. These two fine players were the first to be capped from the St. Mary's Club, and they were to establish a precedent for several more in the years ahead. Hickie had taken over from Goodall who, in the summer of 1970, decided to turn professional with Workington Town, a decision that stunned the rugby union fraternity—and not just in Ireland— and removed from the scene one of the best prospects in the game.

In the summer of 1971, the Lions went to New Zealand and Ireland was well represented on the side. McLoughlin, Sean Lynch, Willie John McBride, Mick Hipwell, Fergus Slattery and Mike Gibson were all in the Lions party and glory beckoned for the side captained by John Dawes.

Gibson, McBride and Lynch all played in the historic test series won by the Lions, while injury forced McLoughlin and Hipwell to return home early; yet it had been freely acknowledged, not least by the Lions coach Carwyn James, that McLoughlin had played a major part in the forward strategy that proved so crucial to the Lions' victories. Slattery, too, had been selected in a test, although he had to withdraw due to illness; but the experience he gained was to prove invaluable on another foreign field three years later.

Ireland full back and captain Tom Kiernan being chaired off the field by jubilant followers after Ireland had beaten Wales.

ENTER POLITICS

WHATEVER THE political differences that divide Ireland, in rugby terms the country has always been a united force. The Orangeman stands shoulder to shoulder with the Dublin Catholic on the terraces at Lansdowne Road and urges on the men in green. It was therefore extremely sad that political influences should have caused major disruption of the 1972 championship.

The troubles in Northern Ireland had been acute since 1969, but rugby went on, clubs from the north travelling south and clubs from the south regularly travelling north, despite the unhappy state of affairs in the north.

Then came an incident that changed the face of rugby football for a period and threatened to disrupt the international scene. Thirteen people were killed in the city of Derry on a Sunday afternoon in controversial circumstances and feelings ran high in Ireland. The British Embassy was burned down in Dublin when some people broke free from a protest march. However unfortunate and ill advised that happening, the actions of a very small minority, Dublin had been markedly free from incident, and the attack on the embassy naturally caused resentment in Britain.

Meanwhile things had never looked better for Ireland on the rugby field. Ireland went to France with five new caps in the side and won a great victory, to end 20 barren years of effort at Colombes, then the French home ground. But if five of the players were new, one was an old stager. Ireland, in an inspired move, decided to bring Kevin Flynn back in the centre. He had not played for Ireland since 1966 and many doubted the wisdom of the decision, but it proved to be a tremendous success. Among the new caps on the side in France were two of the young players who had been taken to the Argentine, scrum half John Moloney and right wing

Tom Grace. Other newcomers were Stewart McKinney on the flank, Wallace McMaster on the left wing and Con Feighery in the second row.

One could really say of that Irish team that it had the blend of youth and experience, for Kiernan had defied the prophets of gloom and was back to lead the side; then there were Ken Kennedy, McBride, McLoughlin, Flynn and Gibson, who between them had won well over 200 caps. The combination proved potent and the win in France was a tremendous boost.

As circumstances decreed, the second match was also away, at Twickenham, and here Ireland won a famous victory, with Flynn getting a marvellous try in injury time to beat England, Bob Hiller included. The enthusiasm in Ireland was tremendous. Two away wins and two home games to come—surely that elusive Triple Crown and Championship were on the horizon. Then enter politics.

Just before the game with England, there were rumours that Scotland were reluctant to come to Dublin, but the Four Home Unions decreed that there was no reason why the Ireland–Scotland match should not go ahead as scheduled.

The Scots still showed reluctance and Welsh voices were being added to the doubters. Eventually a delegation from the I.R.F.U. travelled to Edinburgh to meet the Scottish Rugby Union and offer assurance that the Scots would be quite safe. The Irish delegation was, to say the least, eminent and included a Judge, Charles Conroy, a vice president of the I.R.F.U. at the time, the president Dom Dineen, Ronnie Dawson, and the two international Board members Harry McKibbin and Sinclair Irwin, both as it happened from Ulster. Their pleas fell on deaf ears and Scotland refused to travel. Wales followed suit and so Ireland's chances perished on the altar of political expediency. Ireland refused to play the matches outside Dublin, secure in the knowledge that to do otherwise would have been to agree that Dublin was unsafe, which it patently was not as subsequent events proved.

Quite apart from the acute disappointment for Ireland and the lost chance to win the Triple Crown, there was the not inconsiderable revenue factor. The loss to the I.R.F.U. of the gate receipts from two home games was a considerable financial blow in a country where the revenue from the international matches is vital and really the only source of income for the I.R.F.U.

A friend in need is a friend indeed, and in stepped the French. They agreed to travel to Dublin to play Ireland in April and got a tremendous reception and

Kevin Flynn, recalled to the Ireland side after six years' absence, scores a famous try at Twickenham in 1972 to win the match against England. Mike Gibson is behind Flynn with the England outside half Alan Old on the ground.

a thorough beating for good measure, but that scarcely mattered. What was really relevant was that the I.R.F.U. had proved their point.

It was proved again when the All Blacks came to Dublin in the early part of the 1972–73 season. There were suggestions that the seventh All Blacks would refuse to travel, but the New Zealanders would have none of that and fulfilled all four fixtures, including one in Belfast.

For the international at Lansdowne Road, Ireland still had Flynn in the centre and got a very honourable 10–10 draw, the best result ever achieved by Ireland against the All Blacks. A try by Tom Grace near the end gave Ireland the draw and Barry McGann's conversion from the right touchline looked to be going over the bar; but it veered inches wide at

Ray McLoughlin, one of the greatest prop forwards of the modern era, seen here in action against the All Blacks in 1973, supported by his colleagues Ken Kennedy (right) and Jim Davidson.

the last minute to save the All Blacks' unbeaten record. No Irish side, provincial or national, had ever beaten the tourists, although Munster had almost succeeded in a match four days before the inter-national. With the game in its seventh minute of injury time Munster led 3-0, but the concession of a penalty gave the All Blacks the chance to draw at Musgrave Park.

Now the old arguments about Dublin being a safe place for internationals seemed dead and buried, but a section of the British Press started a campaign to stop England travelling to Dublin. The Rugby Union President, Dick Kingswell, made it absolutely clear that he was in favour of England playing in

Dublin and, following a meeting in the Hilton Hotel in London, called a Press conference and spelled out the message that England would travel to Dublin as England always had and, if necessary, would be prepared to go down the line to pick a side if individual players objected to travelling. As it happened, the England players did not object and England came, much to the disgust of some rugby correspondents. The answer came loud and clear when the England team ran onto the Lansdowne Road pitch to the greatest reception ever given a visiting side. The whole crowd gave England a standing ovation that lasted for several minutes, and some of the England players stated afterwards that they had never known anything like it. Ireland won the match, but this was really not the important factor. England had proved that the game goes on, as Dickie Kingswell had stated so accurately a few weeks previously.

That evening, at the after-match dinner, the England captain John Pullin made the immortal statement that has gone into the folklore of the game. 'We may not,' he said, 'be very good, but at least we turn up.'

Ireland travelled to Scotland and Wales to play their fixtures, and so the championship was back on an even keel again, a situation that was just as it should be.

Dawson had by now served three years as coach and had been replaced by Syd Millar, whose first season of 1973 was not a great success, wins over England and France being balanced by defeats at the hands of Scotland and Wales.

The game against Scotland was notable for one thing: it was Kiernan's last match for Ireland and his 54th, a truly remarkable record. He excelled himself by scoring a try that day at Murrayfield, only his second for Ireland. He was dropped for the visit to Cardiff and replaced by Tony Ensor of Wanderers. So Kiernan had come to the end of the line. Only one man had played more internationals, Colin Meads of New Zealand, who won 55 caps; no man in history before or since had scored more points for Ireland, 158. In addition Kiernan had captained Ireland on 24 occasions, an all-time record. The captaincy now passed to Willie John McBride, Kiernan's long-time team colleague and close friend.

Kiernan left the scene without having helped Ireland to win a Triple Crown or a championship, but he had figured in some record achievements, such as the win over the Springboks and the test victory over Australia in Sydney in 1967. He had also captained the Lions. It was no mean legacy to leave behind.

Argentina made their first visit to Dublin in the autumn of 1973 and Ireland won the test match. Indeed Argentina won only one of four matches played, as they lost to Ulster at Ravenhill and to Munster in Thomond Park. Their only win was achieved against Connacht in Galway.

Tom Grace scores a try in the last minute against New Zealand in Dublin in 1973—a score which gave Ireland a 10-10 draw; the best result achieved by Ireland against the All Blacks.

CHAMPIONS AGAIN

KIERNAN HAD gone and so had Flynn when the 1974 championship started, and the beginning was not one that suggested impending glory for the Irish. Ireland travelled to France, this time to Parc des Princes, now the French home ground in the heart of Paris—a city that had proved anything but gay for the Irish.

Ireland had rebuilt their back line. Moloney was firmly established at scrum half and Gibson in the centre, but McGann had lost out to the Lansdowne outside half Mick Quinn, who had won his first cap against France the previous season. Irish sprint champion Vincent Becker displaced Grace on the right wing in a controversial selection.

Most of the old warriors were still in the pack, but to them was added a big man from Kerry in the second row. Moss Keane was a recent recruit to the rugby game, having concentrated his early sporting energies on playing Gaelic football, both in his native county and as a student at University College Cork.

Once he qualified, he moved to Dublin and joined the Lansdowne club, and here the promise he had revealed in a brief rugby career at University College came to fruition. After some impressive displays for Munster he was named as McBride's second row partner for the game in Paris in 1974.

It was not a winning debut for Keane who did well nonetheless as Ireland only narrowly went down.

For the game against Wales in Dublin, McKinney was dropped and replaced by Shay Deering of Garryowen, whose selection maintained a great family tradition: both his father Seamus and his uncle Mark had also played for Ireland. He was in an Ireland side that drew 9–9 with Wales, thus denting Triple Crown ambitions for both sides; Ireland, with two matches played, had only one point, scarcely a position from which to win the championship.

Willie John McBride was not despondent, however, and believed that Ireland had a reasonable side. 'We should definitely have beaten Wales and I felt quite confident about our journey to Twickenham,' he says in retrospect. 'At that period, away wins were very scarce in the series and a pattern was being established of teams winning at home and of being beaten away. In fact, our win at Twickenham in 1972 was the last recorded by an away side between 1972 and 1974. I nonetheless felt we had a great chance of beating England and we did, but in some respects we made heavy weather of it. We built a big lead and then England outside half Alan Old gradually eroded our lead with a great display of place kicking. But we held on for a good win and our chances of at least sharing the title were bright as we had Scotland to come in the last game.'

In fact, that win over England was clinched by 26 points to 21, a record aggregate score for an Ireland–England match. Moreover, it was Ireland who scored the tries, no fewer than four of them to England's one. Old kicked five penalty goals and a conversion. Gibson scored two tries for Ireland, Ensor one, and the big man who now occupied the number eight berth, Terry Moore from Highfield, got one.

'We should not have allowed England back into that match, for we had it won,' said McBride. 'Bob Hiller had gone by now, but Alan Old was taking over from him and, at one point in the closing stages I thought, not again, surely we are not going to be beaten by a place kicker at Twickenham again.'

If the experienced pack was the cornerstone of the Irish side that afternoon, the backs did splendidly and McBride stressed their contribution. 'The backs really came up well that afternoon. Mike Gibson was at his brilliant best, and that was incomparable at that stage of his career. England just did not have a man of comparable quality behind the scrum that day.'

That away win was to prove crucial as events

Willie John McBride in jubilant mood after the Lions won the Third Test against South Africa in Port Elizabeth in 1974, and so clinched the series. On McBride's left is Gordon Brown, his second row partner.

unfolded in the championship. Ireland beat Scotland in Dublin by 9–6 in a rather scrappy and unimpressive game and so, in a period of seven years, had lost just one match on home soil, to England in 1971. The Scots might have got at least a draw that afternoon. Ireland, with an appreciable breeze at their backs, led 9–0 at the interval, but the Scots dominated the second period and it was the great defensive powers of Gibson in the centre that really saved Ireland. His attacking capacity had been central to fashioning victory over England, and now the rounded nature

of his many-sided talents were demonstrated when the need arose for qualities of a different dimension.

So Ireland ended the Championship with five points and stood at the top of the Championship table with two games still to be played, England v. Wales at Twickenham and Scotland v. France at Murrayfield. Both were scheduled for the same afternoon, March 16th. Both Wales and France could beat Ireland's total of points if they won, and both were favoured to do just that. This time, fate came down on Ireland's side, for England beat Wales and Scotland beat France. Ireland had won the title, 'with a little help from their friends' as McBride put it in his own inimitable way. 'Yet,' he added, 'we were due a little luck and it was great to win it. It made up for the lost chance in 1972. My one regret was that Tom Kiernan did not share in the success, but several of the old hands did'.

Willie John McBride leads Ireland out against England at Twickenham in 1974 to win his 56th cap, a world record at the time.

Mike Gibson has England wing Peter Squires in indecisive mood during the match at Twickenham in 1974. Gibson scored two tries that afternoon when Ireland won 26–21, the highest scoring match in history between the two countries.

McBride, in his first full season as Ireland's captain, had led his side to their first Championship victory in 23 years, so it came as no surprise to most people when he was named to captain the Lions side to tour South Africa in the summer of 1974. He was an extremely popular choice and, with his great friend and Ballymena clubmate Syd Millar named as coach to the Lions, the Irish influence was considerable.

Ireland's success was reflected too in the composition of the side to travel to South Africa, a journey made in the midst of considerable controversy, for the protests against apartheid were now more vociferous than ever.

McBride led a side that contained seven Irish players. They were, in addition to the captain, Fergus Slattery, Stewart McKinney, Ken Kennedy, John Moloney, Tom Grace and Dick Milliken.

Gibson informed the selectors that he was not available for business reasons, as did Ray McLoughlin. The great Welsh wing Gerald Davies was another to opt out. The prophets of gloom suggested that without these players, the Lions would be in trouble in South Africa where no Lions side of the century had won a test series.

McBride proved them wrong. He led a tour of unprecedented success, taking the team through South Africa unbeaten and winning the test series 3–0, with the final test being drawn in Johannesburg in controversial circumstances. Slattery scored a perfectly good try in the closing stages that would have given the Lions victory and a 100 per cent record, but it was disallowed by the South African referee. Filmed evidence subsequently proved that the decision was incorrect.

But the Lions had hammered the Springboks in a way few imagined possible, and McBride's captaincy was acclaimed for what it was—brilliant. Slattery and Milliken played in all four tests with McBride, and Grace, who had been troubled by an ankle injury for much of the early part of the tour, emerged as the top try scorer. Gibson joined the touring party midway through as a replacement for Alan Old who received a severe knee injury, but so well did Milliken and his Scottish centre partner Ian McGeechan play, that Gibson did not get into the test side.

Never in history had a Springboks pack taken such a beating as that inflicted by the 1974 Lions unit.

The Ireland side that drew with Wales in Dublin in 1974 when Ireland regained the International Championship after twenty-three years. Back row (l. to r.): J. West (touch judge), P. Lavery, M. Keane, T. Moore, F. Slattery, S. Deering, A. Ensor, K. Pattinson (R.F.U. referee). Seated: D. Milliken, K. Kennedy, M. Gibson, W. J. McBride (capt.), V. Becker, R. McLoughlin, S. Lynch. In front: M. Quinn, J. Moloney.

ONE HUNDRED YEARS ON

T HE 1974-75 season was the centenary year for the Irish Rugby Football Union, and appropriately Ireland celebrated it as international champions. Things had come a long way since the mid-Victorian era, when a group of students at Trinity College had started it all. At that time, rugby was the preserve of the very few in Ireland; now the game had spread right through the country and, if the main areas of population, such as the cities of Dublin, Belfast, Galway, Cork and Limerick, were the strongholds, then there had been a vast growth in the rural areas and a tremendous enthusiasm for the game.

The I.R.F.U. made elaborate plans to celebrate the centenary and, in true Irish fashion, the celebrations started early and went on late. Ireland met a President's XV in September, a side drawn from all the main rugby playing nations, and caps were awarded for that encounter which was played in a downpour. I suppose it was apt in a way that it should end in a draw.

The All Blacks came on a centenary tour to Ireland, playing in all four provinces and then against Ireland in an international in Dublin, and rather spoiled the party by winning readily, giving a fine display of controlled rugby. The only blot on the tour was a bad head injury sustained by one of the Leinster forwards, Kevin Mays. Winner of four caps in 1973, Mays received a kick that severely damaged one of his ears. That apart, the tour was a great success and the All Blacks most worthy guests for so notable an occasion.

The traditional four countries match brought the celebrations to an end in April, but the centenary was not blessed by an Irish win in the Championship.

The season's opening was encouraging enough, with a 12-9 win over England in Dublin, for which the man mainly responsible was the Ireland outside half Billy McCombe. He had earned a dramatic recall to the ranks after winning one cap in 1968 in Paris, when a student at Trinity College Dublin. Now good form for Ulster, where he was assisting the Bangor club, saw him summoned to the colours, and he scored eight of Ireland's points in a match in which Gibson again played brilliantly. Scotland ended Irish Triple Crown ambitions with a great 20-13 win at Murrayfield and then Ireland hammered France in Dublin by 25 points to six. The match was notable for a try by McBride, the only try he scored for Ireland in his career.

The measure of McBride's popularity was demonstrated when the crowd, standing at the corner where McBride crossed the French line, invaded the pitch and draped the Irish flag around the big man's shoulders. It was an emotional moment. In fact never again would they see McBride wear an Ireland jersey at Lansdowne Road, for, after Ireland took a severe beating from a magnificent Welsh side at the Arms Park, McBride decided that he had come to the end of the international trail. A few months after that match McBride announced his retirement from representative rugby, and when he made that decision, he had won more caps than any man in the history of the game. He had played 63 times for Ireland, made a record five Lions tours, played in 17 test matches for the Lions (an all-time record), captained the most successful Lions side of the century and led Ireland to its first championship win in 23 years. He led the Ireland–Scotland side against England–Wales in the centenary match in Dublin, the last hurrah for one of the greatest forwards ever to grace the rugby scene, and unquestionably one of the greatest of all captains.

On the night of the four countries match, the I.R.F.U. held a banquet in the Shelbourne Hotel, Dublin, a gathering that included the most eminent figures in the game. Notable among them was Sir Wavell Wakefield who made a memorable speech, putting the rugby game into its true perspective. Dr. Danie Craven, the President of the South African Rugby Board, also spoke, as did the president of Ireland, at the time Dr. Cearbail ODalaig.

The International Board paid the I.R.F.U. the signal tribute of holding their annual gathering in Dublin, where the first seeds for the foundation of the Board had been laid, and the I.R.F.U. held an international medical congress there.

Ballymena's two most famous sons, Willie John McBride and Syd Millar, outside the room in the Ballymena clubhouse named in their honour.

The Combined Ireland and President's World XV photographed prior to the special game arranged to mark the I.R.F.U. centenary, which took place at Lansdowne Road in September 1974.

62

Ireland v. the President's World XV. The great Welsh scrum half Gareth Edwards makes a break for the President's XV as Sean Lynch and Terry Moore of Ireland attempt to halt Edwards' progress.

Terry Moore, who won 12 caps for Ireland at number eight, attempts to sweep past the All Blacks scrum half Syd Going in the international at Lansdowne Road in November 1974.

Willie John McBride gathers the ball in the match against New Zealand at Lansdowne Road. The All Blacks made a special tour to Ireland to mark the I.R.F.U. centenary. Another forward, Sean Lynch, is on hand to offer his support to McBride.

John Moloney, *capped 27 times for Ireland (23 at scrum half and four on the wing), seen here in the colours of the combined Ireland–Scotland team against England–Wales in the special four countries match at Lansdowne Road in April 1975, to mark the I.R.F.U. centenary. Moloney is supported by Ian McGeechan as Alan Old and Mervyn Davies of England–Wales close in.*

Two great players in opposition. Mike Gibson, playing for Ireland–Scotland against England–Wales in Dublin in 1975, kicks clear as Mervyn Davies closes in.

The I.R.F.U. also decided to hold an All Ireland Club Championship which was won by St. Mary's College. Now very much a power in the land, the college was sending out some of the finest of Irish players since the breakthrough had been made just five years earlier, when Denis Hickie and Sean Lynch became the first players from the club to win caps.

The President of the I.R.F.U. for centenary year was Harry McKibbin, a man who had given tremendous service to the game as player and legislator. He had been capped in 1938, went on a Lions tour that year and, like many another, had his career interrupted by the war. His brother Des was capped, and Harry was to see his two sons, Harry junior and Alistair, follow the family traditions by playing for Ireland. He is still one of Ireland's International Board representatives and epitomises the many characteristics that have marked Irish rugby in over a century of honest endeavour.

The centenary celebrations, and their many sided nature, gave the game added impetus in Ireland, but few can have visualised that they would preface lean times for the Irish in the field of international competition, if not in terms of the general propagation of the game in the country.

Tom Grace, who shares the cap record with Alan Duggan for a wing threequarter with 25 appearances for Ireland, scores a try for Ireland–Scotland against England–Wales in the I.R.F.U. centenary match at Lansdowne Road in April 1975.

HARD TIMES

three years earlier. Meates faced a tough task—how tough we would soon discover.

Ireland had a match against Australia in January 1976, which seemed likely to be good preparation for the championship; instead it compounded the problems for the selectors. Nor was Ireland's first match at 'B' level of much use or significance. That took place in December 1975 against France in Dublin and Ireland won a very poor match by 9—6, all the points coming from penalty goals. The match was notable too for the fact that the referee, Alan Welsby of England, sent no fewer than four players off the field, two from both sides.

When Ireland faced Australia, the selectors yet

THE CENTENARY celebrations over, one very tangible legacy was left behind, and that concerned schools rugby, always so vital for Ireland. The I.R.F.U. decided, as part of the celebrations, to play a schools international against England. The game, which was played at Lansdowne Road, was a considerable success, even if the attendance was not comparable to the huge crowds that annually patronise the schools cup competitions in the provinces.

Since centenary year, however, Ireland has put sides in the field regularly at schools level and in the summer of 1980 sent a team to Australia.

There was a notable change in the Ireland national side at top level, however, when the centenary celebrations had ended. When the campaign for 1975–76 started, some of the old hands were missing. McBride had retired; gone too were the entire front row of Ray McLoughlin, Ken Kennedy and Sean Lynch. So Ireland had lost four world class forwards. All four had served Ireland, and indeed the Lions, with great distinction and would be a severe loss.

There was another loss that was completely unexpected and represented a very serious blow indeed. Dick Milliken, who had played so well for the Lions in 1974 and whose performances in the centre for Ireland, in partnership with Mike Gibson, suggested great possibilities, received a very serious ankle injury that, in the end, terminated his career many years before its time. He made some valiant efforts to return to the top sphere, but to no avail.

Ireland had a new coach now too. Syd Millar had served the usual three year period and retired at the end of the 1975 championship. He was succeeded by Roly Meates, a man who had been at the heart of the coaching crusade in Leinster and who had been a candidate for the national job when Millar got it

again revealed their facility for going back in time, as it were. In an effort to solve the second row problems caused by McBride's retirement, they recalled Mick Molloy who, to the surprise of many people, had not played at international level for five years, despite the succession of partners McBride had been given before Moss Keane emerged on the scene. The return of the London Irish man was not a success, and indeed the most encouraging aspect of the Irish pack now was the form shown by the number eight, Willie Duggan from the Blackrock College club. He had come in the previous season and his play suggested the possibility of a fine career. That promise has been well fulfilled subsequently.

Kennedy's place as hooker went to another Blackrock man, John Cantrell, who was preferred to Pat Whelan of Garryowen, for so long Kennedy's understudy. Whelan had won two caps the previous season before Kennedy regained his place; now with Kennedy gone, it was to Cantrell the selectors turned.

In the front row, the selectors brought in two men well over 30: Paddy Agnew from Ulster, and

Mike Gibson makes another break for Ireland, this time against Wales in Dublin during the match in 1976, as J. P. R. Williams and Mervyn Davies attempt to halt his progress.

Roly Meates (left) and Tom Grace, respectively coach and captain of Ireland during the lean years of 1976 and 1977.

Feidhlim McLoughlin, brother of Ray. Feidhlim, who played his rugby with the Northern club in England, was a good durable prop who can hardly have been expecting the call when it came. Many old hands had gone, but it seemed as if the selectors were determined to bring in even older replacements. It was an extraordinary choice, that pack that faced Australia.

In contrast, the half backs selected against Australia were very young. John Robbie from Trinity College was named at scrum half and his partner was Ollie Campbell, a young player from Old Belvedere. Both had been excellent schools players, if short on senior experience. In fact, Campbell was a last-minute choice, as Barry McGann, who had re-established his claim to the outside half position, had had to withdraw.

So the line-up against Australia in many ways emphasised the fluid nature of Irish rugby at the time, and Ireland lost 20—10 and could scarcely complain about the result. Campbell, later to leave such an indelible imprint on the scene, had a dreadful afternoon with his kicking and missed three in the early stages. One wondered at the wisdom of the new captain Mike Gibson, giving the kicks to the youngster. Campbell was not to appear on the scene again for three years. Robbie was retained for the visit to Paris when yet again major alterations were made. Slattery, sadly out of form, was dropped and Deering and McKinney were in the back row, while Phil Orr, a prop from Old Wesley, was named for his first cap, but only after the original choice had been forced to withdraw. Ian McIlrath, a sturdy centre from Ballymena, was Gibson's partner in the centre.

Ireland's problems were underlined when France inflicted a dreadful 26–3 hammering.

It was all change again for the visit of Wales, and one of the decisions taken after the match in Paris was to give the captaincy to Tom Grace, instead of Gibson who was clearly unhappy in the role of leader and asked to be relieved of it. That request did no more, however, than pre-empt the selectors' thoughts, for Gibson would have lost the captaincy in any case. In turning to Grace, the selectors opted for a man

The enthusiastic scenes at Thomond Park, Limerick, after Munster had beaten the All Blacks 12–0 on October 31st, 1978—a red letter day in the history of the game in Ireland. In the foreground are three of the Munster heroes, Moss Keane, Donal Canniffe and Greg Barrett.

Ireland v. France, 1975. Willie John McBride scoring a try for Ireland at Lansdowne Road, in his last international. It was the only try McBride scored for Ireland in 63 appearances.

who was extremely competitive and had the respect of his colleagues. Keane had another new partner in Ronnie Hakin, from C.I.Y.M.S. in Belfast, Brendan Foley having been tried out in Paris.

Prior to the match against Wales, approaches were made to McBride and Ray McLoughlin to make themselves available, but both wisely resisted in the belief that it would not serve the cause of Irish rugby in the long term. Denials about the approaches were made, but carried no weight. The match against Wales saw Ireland crash 34–9, after leading in the early stages. Wales were rampant in the second half, clearly well on their way to the Triple Crown, and they left Ireland not even a crumb of comfort.

When Ireland travelled to England, it was all change yet again, and when Duggan was forced to withdraw, it seemed as if the chances, already rated slim, were gone. He was replaced by Harry Steele from Ballymena, a fine forward whose performances had not yet earned him recognition. As it transpired, it was not until two years later that he made his place secure. Ireland got an unexpected and very welcome win at Twickenham over an England side

that was in even greater disarray than Ireland's. Then it was back to base when Scotland came to Dublin and won 15–6. Five matches, one win and four defeats was not exactly the ideal backdrop for a tour to New Zealand which was scheduled in the summer.

Nevertheless that tour took place, and Ireland did better than expected, winning four matches and losing three, including the Wellington test by 11–3. It was in some respects an unlucky defeat. Ireland then went to Fiji and won the only match played, so the return from the tour was encouraging.

Meates had worked hard on the forward strategy and gained reasonable success as he sought to counter the great strength of New Zealand forward play, notably rucks and mauls, and to cut down the driving of the New Zealanders up front. Robbie had a fine tour, as did McGann and Grace behind the scrum, where Gibson shone yet again in a land where his ability is highly regarded.

The tour did not, however, really do Irish rugby much good in the final analysis, and the 1977 campaign was a total disaster. Ireland lost all four matches and made a multitude of changes, bringing in new caps who were clearly not ready for this level of competition. Gibson was put back at out half after McGann broke his leg in the trial; then Quinn was recalled and Gibson restored to the centre. The forward play too had deteriorated again and clearly Ireland had moved no nearer to solving the problems that had existed since the last championship success in 1974. In addition, place kicking was sadly deficient.

Meates was the first victim, for he was not reappointed for the 1978 campaign, the selectors turned to Noel Murphy to do the job. Murphy was a selector and had been one for two seasons; now he had the added responsibility of being coach as well. It was Meates' misfortune to be coach when Ireland had major problems; in many respects he was not helped by the selectors' approach. Few envied Murphy his task. The poor state of Ireland's international prestige had been well reflected in the Irish representation on the Lions tour to New Zealand the previous summer. Ireland had three players selected, Gibson, Orr and Duggan. Keane was subsequently called into the side when Geoff Wheel of Wales withdrew. Duggan, alone, managed to win a regular test place and I do not think Ireland had any reason to complain.

When the Ireland team to meet Scotland in Dublin in January 1978 was named, it contained one major surprise. John Moloney, who had been a regular in the side for much of the seventies, was recalled at scrum half and given the captaincy, and his new partner was Tony Ward, from Garryowen. Ward had played for Ireland at 'B' level and his performances for his province, Munster, and for his club were attracting great attention. The back line was completely reconstructed now, with Harry McKibbin's son Alistair, who had made his debut the previous year, in the centre. He was partnered by Paul McNaughton, an accomplished soccer player of amateur international status, with Grace and another new man, Alfred MacLennan, on the wings. Whelan had regained the hooking berth the previous season and was propped by Orr and a new cap, Mick Fitzpatrick, from Wanderers.

Slattery was back in favour by now too, and Donal Spring, a man from a distinguished sporting family and a student at Trinity College, was in the second row with Keane.

Ireland beat Scotland by 12-9 and it was mainly thanks to Ward, who had made a most impressive debut and kicked eight points. Quite apart from his place kicking, his general tactical kicking was of the highest order. A new star had surely arrived on the scene.

Ireland went to France for a match on a ground covered in ice and clearly unplayable. Ireland lost most unluckily by 10-9, although Ward, Moloney and Duggan played brilliantly, as did Ensor at full back. Once more Ward kicked three penalty goals. His success ratio was a remarkable 80 per cent from the penalty chances and that contrasted with a success rate of around 30 per cent prior to his arrival. Penalty failings along with other deficiencies had cost Ireland a heavy price.

Wales came to Dublin in search of a third successive Triple Crown and were extremely fortunate to win 20-16, clinching victory in the dying moments of a tremendously hard game. Ward scored 12 of Ireland's points with Moloney getting a try, and later it was again Ward who scored all Ireland's nine points in the 15-9 defeat at Twickenham.

Ireland had won only one of four matches, but there was vast improvement in the general level of performance and certainly Ireland might well have won three of the four games. The biggest single difference was the presence of Ward. He scored 38 points in four appearances to equal the highest mark by any individual in the championship series. Besides that achievement, he was named as 'European Player of the Year', an honour that was thoroughly earned. Ireland had played Mike Gibson on the wing in this campaign, and his natural aptitude revealed

itself in his new position. The pack was much better too with Steele now Keane's partner, Spring having sustained a bad knee injury. One casualty of that campaign was Grace, who lost his place when Gibson was put on the wing. Grace played 25 times for Ireland to equal Alan Duggan's record number of appearances.

There was reason enough for optimism at the start of the 1979 championship, and Ward represented a very big part of that optimism. The All Blacks came to Ireland in the autumn of 1978, and on October 31st Irish rugby had one of its greatest days. That afternoon at Thomond Park, Munster achieved what they had so often threatened but so unluckily failed to do: they beat the All Blacks and did it in the most comprehensive and impressive manner possible. Munster won 12-0 with Ward the mastermind behind the scrum, and he had a personal contribution of eight points.

The Munster team tackled like demons that afternoon to thrill a capacity attendance in the great rugby city of Limerick. Tom Kiernan had coached the Munster side and he had read the All Blacks' hand brilliantly. Munster took them out forward, did not concede penalties and defended with tremendous effect.

The scenes at the end of the game were memorable. The Munster players were carried off the field in triumph, the first and to date the only Irish side ever to beat the All Blacks. The New Zealanders were gracious in their defeat and generous in their praise for a worthy victory.

It was the ideal tonic for Ireland who faced the tourists in the international the following Saturday. For that game Moloney, who had done so much the previous season to lift the Irish fortunes, was dropped and replaced by the Ulster player Colin Patterson at scrum half. The captaincy was given to Shay Deering who thereby created a record for St. Mary's College. Following in the steps of Grace and Moloney from the same club, St. Mary's College thus gave Ireland three successive captains, a feat no other club had attained.

Ireland lost to New Zealand by 10 points to six, but Patterson did justify his selection as Ward's partner. Once more Ward scored Ireland's points, as the Irish backs made poor use of possession and Mike Gibson, in the centre, looked to have come to the end of the line.

Ireland opened their 1979 campaign at home to France and drew 9-9 with Ward the only scorer. Yet, but for a misunderstanding by Ward, Ireland would surely have won. The home team had been awarded

The Munster team that scored the famous victory over the All Blacks and became the only Irish side in history to beat them, as well as the first Irish side to prevent them from scoring. Back row (l. to r.): Sean Gavin (President of the Munster Branch I.R.F.U.), John Cole (touch judge), Gerry McLoughlin, Les White, Moss Keane, Donal Spring, Colm Tucker, Pat Whelan, Brendan Foley, Corris Thomas (Wales, Referee), Martin Walsh (touch judge). Front row (l. to r.): Tony Ward, Christy Cantillon, Moss Finn, Seamus Dennison, Donal Canniffe (capt.), Greg Barrett, Jimmy Bowen, Larry Moloney.

a differential penalty in front of the French posts and Ward, not realising he could retreat as far back as he liked, elected to take the kick from near the posts and had it charged down. He had played much of the match with concussion which did not help. It was a pity, but a draw was a reasonable enough start to the season.

Ireland then went to Wales and scored 21 points, the highest ever by an Irish side in Wales; even so they lost, thanks to some incredible mistakes near their own line. Ward scored 13 points that afternoon and Wales will never have a luckier victory.

Ensor was gone now and his replacement at fullback was Dick Spring from Lansdowne, a brother of Donal, one of the most promising of the younger school of forwards. Dick Spring had a most unhappy afternoon in Cardiff, as did Colin Patterson, yet both survived for the game against England which Ireland won 12-7 in Dublin, in what many consider to have been Ward's greatest game for his country. He was a mainline target for the England back row and frequently late tackled, but in the first half, when the Irish were under pressure, he was the mainstay; in the second he was the match winner, and a dropped goal in that second period was one of the best ever seen at Lansdowne Road.

Ireland played indifferently against Scotland at Murrayfield and drew 11–11. They had lost just one game in the Championship, to Wales, so things were definitely looking up.

For the game against Scotland, Mike Gibson surprisingly appeared playing on the right wing. Prior to the start of the championship, he had informed the selectors that he had retired and did not wish to be considered again. Terry Kennedy of St. Mary's was Ireland's regular on the wing, but he had influenza and withdrew the day before the game, and so Gibson was called in. In fact Gibson's presence was due to a doubt about Alistair McKibbin who, however, came through the training session on the Thursday before the match. Terry Kennedy was feeling unwell at the session and not surprisingly, withdrew on the Friday in Edinburgh, so Gibson was named to play on the wing, returning to the international field just a matter of a few months after his decision to retire.

Ireland had done quite well in the 1979 championship and things had improved greatly since the bad days of 1977. Now another great adventure lay ahead, but few could have visualised the degree of controversy that was about to break out on the far side of the world.

CONTROVERSY AND ACHIEVEMENT

THE IRELAND party to tour Australia was selected, and Ollie Campbell, who had had one game in 1976 against Australia, was named among the backs after some very impressive displays for his club in the Leinster Cup campaign. A severe knee injury sustained in September had prevented him from playing much rugby that season, but his slow return to fitness was followed by those good displays for his club and he was named, presumably as Ward's understudy. Ward had just been elected 'European Player of the Year' for the second time and had won that distinction by a record margin in a record poll.

Jack Coffey, a former President of the I.R.F.U., was named as manager, Murphy was coach and Slattery was captain. Together they made up the tour's management structure.

Prior to the tour, Coffey, a man with a long connection with the game, whose father had also been an I.R.F.U. president, made some ominous remarks which suggested that he was not among Ward's admirers, but if so he was in a minority, not only in Ireland but throughout the rugby playing world. Murphy, too, had been known to be critical of Ward, although the latter had been the man responsible for much of the success during Murphy's tenure of office. One of the things Ward achieved was a 70 per cent success ratio with his place kicking. Had Ward been playing when Roly Meates was coach, Noel Murphy might have had to wait longer to get the job of coach.

Before the first match in Perth, against Western Australia, Ireland lost a player. Prop forward Ned Byrne, from Blackrock, a man who was contesting the tight head berth with Mick Fitzpatrick and Gerry McLoughlin, from the Shannon club, was knocked down by a hit and run driver. He sustained a broken leg, so a hasty message was sent for a replacement and Fitzpatrick was summoned. When the team to meet Western Australia was announced, Ward was not in it. The selectors had opted for Campbell, which was a surprise, even allowing for the fact that Western Australia could not be rated among the stronger teams likely to be encountered on tour.

Campbell, in fact, did not have a happy day; although Ireland won easily, he missed the first four kicks he took at goal. It was not until Ireland had the match won that Campbell was restored to kicking duties. Gibson had been named on the wing and did reasonably well.

The next game was against Australian Capital Territory in Canberra and Ward was outside half. He scored 19 points, gave a magnificent display and scored a great try, and Ireland won 35-7. That 19 points effort by Ward against A.C.T. was a record for any Irish player in any match tour or international. The Garryowen man was on form and indeed, a neutral observer at that game commented in his report afterwards that 'Ward made the match worthwhile'. Otherwise it was a sloppy and unconvincing performance from the Irish against mediocre opposition.

The next assignment was against New South Wales in Sydney, a tough task for any touring side. Ward was again outside half, with Gibson once more on the wing. The Irish forwards did extremely well and Ireland built a 16-0 lead, with Ward getting two penalty goals and a conversion, two of the kicks being from the touchline. Towards the end the Irish faltered, and Gibson had a particularly unhappy game on the wing with his opponent Phil Crowe getting in for two tries, both converted; a match that had seemed already won saw Ireland hanging on grimly in the closing stages, when Ward's great defensive kicking proved crucial.

73

Now it was on to Ballymore and a match against Queensland, the champions of the Australian provincial sides, who had the majority representation in the Australian team.

Campbell was at outside half for this one, with John Moloney, who had travelled as a scrum half, named on the left wing after Alfred MacLennan had withdrawn. Moloney had the pace to play in that position, as well as the football ability and perception.

Ireland won 18–15, with Campbell kicking six penalty goals for a fine individual performance, yet scarcely, as we thought, of sufficient moment to oust Ward. But there was a belief in the party that Campbell might be named in the centre, where there was a problem in finding a partner for Paul McNaughton. Gibson, however, played there against Queensland and did reasonably well, but his powers had clearly diminished. To observers it seemed that, if the selectors wanted to accommodate Ward and Campbell and do so on the basis of current form, then Campbell in the centre and Ward at outside half would be the logical step.

The night before the test team was announced there were reasons to suspect that Ward was under pressure, and Mr. Coffey certainly gave the impression that Ward was about to be dropped. Ward however, was not aware of his peril.

The team travelled to Paradise Bay outside Brisbane for a training session on the Thursday prior to the game, and when the party arrived, Ward was called aside and told he was not in the test side. He was clearly shattered, even though just before the coach reached its destination his club colleague Pat Whelan had tipped him off that he was in grave danger. Whelan had got the information from a journalist who had been present the previous evening, when Mr. Coffey had made his views known about who would be at outside half.

When the team returned to the hotel, Mr. Coffey was asked by two journalists if they could interview Ward; Coffey refused, a decision that surprised the touring Press who had been assured by Coffey and Murphy, prior to the tour, that players would at all times be available for interview, provided that the interviews were cleared by the management. A request to Coffey that Ward be interviewed with the manager and coach present was also turned down.

Ward was clearly upset and his mood had not changed when Murphy called to his room and asked if he would accompany him to a cinema. Perhaps an explanation as to why he had been dropped might have helped Ward more. Never can a man have given so much to an Ireland side and been dropped as a 'reward'. Not surprisingly the news made the front pages in Ireland and elsewhere and one Australian critic even suggested that 'The Irish were surely playing games to confuse the Australians and would play Ward on Sunday'.

The test was a personal triumph for Campbell who scored four penalty goals, a dropped goal and two conversions for 19 points in a great Ireland win by 27 points to 12. Campbell kicked immaculately after nearly missing his first kick at goal. The Irish forwards, too, played magnificently and completely demolished the Australians; Patterson, at their heels, scored two tries as the Australian pack was shoved back near their own line. Moloney played on the left wing and, at full back, Rodney O'Donnell made a superb international debut before being injured in a quite unnecessary late charge and replaced by Frank Ennis.

Ireland did not play a running game; it was a conservative approach and the ball never went beyond the first centre. What Ward might have made of the opportunity one can only speculate; but Campbell certainly made the most of it, so the selectors probably felt justified in their decision—if success is its own justification.

Murphy admitted afterwards that he had spent 'a few very uneasy days before the game wondering if he had made the right decision in dropping Ward'. What most of the rest of us wondered, even in the aftermath of the win, was by what route Murphy, Coffey and Slattery had arrived at the decision to drop Ward and what part Gibson had played in that decision. Coffey, for instance was well known to be a critic of the Garryowen man, while Murphy seemed to vary greatly in his assessment of the player. In 1977, when opposing his selection for Munster to Barry McGann, he had described him as 'second rate', and yet after Ward's great match against England in Dublin in 1979, he had called him 'world class, and a man who represents the future of Irish rugby'. What is very clear is that the Irish rugby establishment seemed to resent the publicity given to Ward.

Ireland went on to beat New South Wales Country Districts to maintain a 100 per cent record, and then lost to Sydney in the second last match when Campbell played at full back with Ward at

(Right): Tony Ward, who kicked thirty-eight points for Ireland in the 1978 Championship to equal the record for any player from any country in the series, in action for Ireland at Lansdowne Road as he kicks three more points for Ireland.

The Ireland squad and officials for the Australian tour in the summer of 1979. This was Ireland's most successful touring side ever. Ireland won both tests on the tour, the only one of the Home Countries to do so in a series in the southern hemisphere. Back row (l. to r.): T. Kennedy, T. Ward, R. O'Donnell, A. MacLennan, O. Campbell, F. Ennis, A. McLean, C. Fitzgerald, C. Patterson. Middle Row (l. to r.): P. Andreucetti, C. Cantillon, E. Byrne, J. O'Driscoll, Dr. R. O'Connell (medical officer), B. Foley, W. Duggan, D. Irwin, G. McLoughlin, P. McNaughton. Seated (l. to r.): P. Whelan, J. Moloney, M. Gibson, J. Coffey (manager), F. Slattery (capt.), N. Murphy (coach), M. Keane, H. Steele, P. Orr.

outside half. Obviously for the second test, Campbell was retained and O'Donnell was fit to return at full back, while Moloney, capped 23 times at scrum half, retained the wing berth in the face of the challenge from MacLennan, now fully fit again.

Ireland won a fine victory in the second test by 9-3, with Campbell again doing a 'Ward' with two dropped goals and a penalty goal. This time the Irish pack did not dominate to the same extent, but they withstood a lot of pressure at the famous Sydney Cricket ground. The crowd here can be partisan and vociferous, and they lived up to both reputations that afternoon when O'Donnell gave one of the best displays ever by an Irish full back.

So the tour was over and Ireland had won the test series 2-0, the best result ever attained by any of the home countries on a tour in the southern hemisphere. Ward returned to Ireland, clearly perplexed by it all, and Campbell emerged as a hero, having gone out as an 'extra'.

A knee injury sustained by Ward ruled him out of consideration for the 1980 campaign until the last two games, when he was named as replacement. Ireland won two and lost two of the championship matches, with Campbell playing brilliantly against Wales in the final match of the campaign. After starting out as favourites, Ireland lost to France in Paris and to England at Twickenham in the first match of the championship. Campbell scored 46 points in the series to set a new record for a player in the championships—all the points coming from kicks.

In that championship some of the players who had made a mark in Australia were in the side, notably hooker Ciaran Fitzgerald and full back Rodney O'Donnell; both seemed set for long careers.

When the Lions party to tour South Africa in the summer was announced, Bill Beaumont, the England captain, was named to lead the tourists, an absolutely correct decision after the manner in which he had led England to the Grand Slam. Ireland supplied both the manager Syd Millar and the coach Noel Murphy for a tour that raised major controversy.

O'Donnell, Campbell, Patterson, O'Driscoll and Colm Tucker were all named in the party, with Tucker, a flanker from Shannon—a surprising choice as he was unable to hold down a regular berth on the Irish side. Many players were not available, including some Irishmen, both on principle and for the reason that they could not get time off from work.

Campbell was injured early on and indeed there were many injuries on that tour. One man called out was Ward, who had not played an international

Tony Ward, surrounded by a host of young admirers after one of his great games for Ireland, against England at Lansdowne Road.

since March 1979. He was named in the team for the first test and scored 18 points, despite taking the field with a badly bruised thigh that kept him out of action for a fortnight after the match. His total in the test at Newlands represented a record for a Lions player in a test match. His absence from the international scene, inexplicable to most observers outside Ireland, became an even greater mystery, while Murphy, who had dismissed him in Australia, was relieved now to be able to call on the Garryowen man when it was expedient.

John Robbie and Phil Orr were also called out during the tour, while for O'Donnell and Patterson it spelled the end of their careers. O'Donnell received a very serious neck injury playing at the Wanderers ground in Johannesburg in the 12th match of the tour against the Junior Springboks. He underwent an operation in South Africa, but then had to have another on his return home and spent almost two months in hospital. Patterson received a dreadful knee injury in the second last match of the tour against Griquas in Kimberley. He suffered damaged knee ligaments and had to be operated on immediately, and he has since played no serious rugby. Altogether it was a costly tour for the Irish, besides being Murphy's last major assignment as a coach, for he had completed his three years with Ireland by the end of the 1980 campaign. He was succeeded by his cousin Kiernan who was about to face those twin but diverse experiences, disaster and triumph.

Kiernan's first task was to prepare the Ireland side to meet Romania in Dublin in November 1980. Once more Ward was left out, but circumstances decreed that he played when Paul McNaughton withdrew and Campbell was moved to centre. Ireland dominated the first half and Ward surpassed himself; he and Campbell combined to put new-comer Frank Quinn in for a great try. Ireland, however, fell away badly in the second period and were rather fortunate, in the end, to get a draw.

Ward was omitted again for the first game of the championship against France in Dublin in January 1981. Campbell was at out half with Robbie as his partner; McNaughton and David Irwin were in the centre. Irwin, who had been on the tour to Australia, had come into the side during the 1980 champion-ship and done well. Quinn and MacLennan were on the wings, and a new cap, Hugo MacNeill from Trinity College, came in at full back.

Ciaran Fitzgerald had damaged a shoulder, so Whelan was back at hooker and Brendan Foley was again Keane's second row partner, with Slattery, Duggan and O'Driscoll forming a very experienced

Ireland scrum half John Robbie in action against Romania at Lansdowne Road in November 1980, while Moss Keane and Ciaran Fitzgerald keep a watching brief. This was Ireland's only meeting with Romania and ended in a draw.

back row. MacNeill marked his arrival on the scene with a great try, but Ireland lost 19–13, fading away in the closing stages.

The selectors decided that it was time to send for Ward again, and he was at outside half against Wales in Cardiff with Campbell in the centre. Ward played splendidly, as did Campbell in the centre. Ireland scored two tries, but nevertheless Wales won 9–8, scoring two penalty goals and a dropped goal, the latter coming in the closing minutes to win the match. Ironically, Ireland had the two best place kickers in the game in their side, but in a very fitful wind they failed to kick one goal. However, Ward had proved his point. A few weeks earlier he had kicked magnificently at the Arms Park in the four countries match arranged to celebrate the Welsh centenary. That afternoon he had scored a record number of points—15—for a four countries match, with a try, four conversions and a penalty goal. Now the ball would not go between the posts for either Ward or Campbell.

England beat Ireland at Lansdowne Road and then Ireland travelled to Scotland and lost again, by a single point in a match played in dreadful conditions. It was a whitewash for Kiernan in his first year as coach, and Ireland faced a tour to South Africa in the summer of 1981, with Paddy Madigan, chairman of the Ireland selectors, as manager.

Controversy raged in Ireland over this tour. In the end, the I.R.F.U. decided that it would go ahead, but it was obvious that the Irish side would be very depleted. Four players refused to travel on grounds of principle. They were MacNeill, Ward, Keane and Donal Spring. In addition Ciaran Fitzgerald, Paul McNaughton and Mick Fitzpatrick were not available for business reasons. Two players, Robbie and second row Gerry Holland from Wanderers, had to give up their jobs to go when their employers refused leave of absence. The tour was contentious in the extreme and, while opinion polls showed that a majority of the Irish public were against the tour, and opinion within rugby itself very divided, the I.R.F.U. stood firm. One player, Michael Gibson from Lansdowne, a big back row forward who had made an impact when he came into the side in 1979, was greatly troubled by injury. He too decided to stay at home when his employers, Guinness, refused leave of absence and also refused to allow him to take annual leave. Robbie, who was also employed by Guinness, took the opposite line and gave up his job.

It was an intimidating background against which to start the tour, and Ireland lost the first match to the Junior Springboks. The opposition ranged

Rodney O'Donnell, full back for Ireland in the two tests against Australia in 1979 and for the Lions against South Africa in the first test in Cape Town in 1980. His career was cut short by a serious neck injury sustained on the Lions tour in 1980.

Philip Orr, with Brendan Foley and Fergus Slattery in support, makes a typical drive against Wales.

against the Irish in most of the other matches was, quite frankly, substandard, and games against such obscure opposition as the South African Mining team, the Gold Cup Selection and the President's Cup selection were meaningless. Ireland overwhelmed them all, marking up huge totals.

In the tests it was South Africa who prevailed, but only just. The Irish were very unlucky and played splendidly in the first Test at Cape Town before going down; while in the second, in Durban, they lost by a point, with Naas Botha, the Springboks outside half, kicking his side to success. Ireland played that second test without Campbell who had broken a bone in his wrist in the first test. Paul Dean, from St.

Mary's College, won his first cap at outside half, while Mick Quinn of Lansdowne was at outside half, having joined the party as a replacement when injury struck. The tour proved conclusively that multiracial rugby in South Africa had not advanced as had been suggested. The opposition faced by the Irish side was its own argument.

So Kiernan's record with Ireland was played six and lost six as he contemplated events for the 1982 championship. It was enough to intimidate the most resolute, but Kiernan insisted that his players were much better than the record suggested, and he was all set to prove that point in 1982.

TRIPLE CROWN GLORY AGAIN

MANY AN historic happening has been fashioned against an unlikely background and exceptional circumstances, and one can certainly so describe the sequence of events in the International Championship series in 1982.

The Australians came to Britain and Ireland in the autumn of 1981, thus affording the teams in the International Championship a fine opportunity to test their strength in a full international before the championship series began. Meanwhile, in Ireland, thoughts turned to the now familiar topic of whether Tony Ward or Ollie Campbell would be at outside half, or whether the selectors would follow the line taken the previous season and accommodate both players. All speculation on that count ended late in September when it was announced that Campbell would not be playing rugby until the new year. He had broken a wrist in South Africa, that had healed well, but just before the start of the season he went to the United States with his club Old Belvedere, and on his return he was ill with an infection causing some weeks lay-off. He had played a lot of rugby since the Australian tour of 1979, going to South Africa in the summer of 1980 with the Lions and back there again in 1981 with Ireland. Those assignments, plus his commitments on the home front, had left him tired and probably a little stale.

A fact not generally known was that after his return from the United States and his subsequent illness, Campbell had decided that he would opt out of representative rugby and had notified Kevin Flynn, the chairman of the Ireland selectors, accordingly. Campbell had also decided that he would play on at club level. Flynn suggested to the player that he should reconsider his planned course and that he should take a rest from the game until after Christmas, reassessing his position thereafter. Flynn felt, quite correctly, that Campbell would benefit considerably from a rest after his strenuous schedule of the previous three years when he was playing rugby winter and summer at home and abroad.

Campbell opted to follow that advice, which ruled him out of consideration for the Interprovincial series and, of course, for Ireland's match against Australia, scheduled for Lansdowne Road early in December.

It was felt too that a return by Campbell in January would not give him much of a chance of mounting a challenge for a place in the national side, at least for the early games in the championship, so Ward was the obvious man for the outside half task against the Wallabies.

Then Ward sustained a knee injury which put him out of action for several weeks, but he recovered in time to play for Munster against the Wallabies, a game scheduled for the Tuesday prior to the international. In the interim, he had proved his fitness in a club game the previous Saturday.

The Australians faced Munster at Musgrave Park in Cork, and once more the Munstermen rose to the occasion to beat a touring side and do it comprehensively. Ward excelled himself. He completely destroyed the Wallabies and gave a display that prompted Kevin Flynn to say, 'I have never seen him play better'. His kicking, tactical and otherwise, was of the highest class.

Ireland failed miserably to do what Munster had done and the Australians won a most worthy victory in the international. The Irish forwards had a marked advantage in the set scrums, but apart from that gave a lethargic display. Ward, in common with most of his backline colleagues, did not have a good day, and the Irish back row of Fergus Slattery, Willie Duggan and John O'Driscoll had a torrid time as Tony Shaw led the Australian pack well.

Ireland had also lost two players, John Robbie and wing Alfred MacLennan having decided to settle in South Africa. Robbie's absence meant that Robbie McGrath of Wanderers was now at scrum half where he had played so very well in the two test matches in South Africa the previous summer, after John Robbie was ruled out through injury.

Phil Orr and Moss Keane, two great Ireland forwards who help win the Triple Crown and Championship in 1982. Keane and Orr have won nearly eighty caps between them, and toured New Zealand with the 1977 Lions.

Tom Kiernan, who captained Ireland a record twenty-four times and is Ireland's leading points scorer in international rugby with one hundred and fifty-eight points, shows the way to his players during a coaching session. He coached Ireland to the Triple Crown and Championship in 1982.

On top of this, Moss Keane, who had refused to travel to South Africa, damaged an ankle playing for Munster against Ulster and he too was ruled out of the game against Australia.

The result, and the manner of the Irish performance against Australia, suggested that Ireland and Tom Kiernan faced a troubled championship. Then, to compound their problems, Fergus Slattery wrote to the selectors and stated that he did not again want to be considered as captain of the side.

Ireland had lost seven successive matches, the worst sequence for 20 years, lost their captain and seemed to be rapidly losing their faith in themselves.

The Irish trial was played before Christmas and Slattery and Keane, to mention just two, were relegated to the possibles. Campbell, of course, had not returned, so Ward was opposed by Hugh Condon, of London Irish. Ward had a 100 per cent record with his kicks, as he had had when playing for Munster against Leinster in the interprovincial decider. The result of that match in Cork, a draw, thus left Leinster champions for the third successive year.

The possibles won the final trial with some of the

The first of the 1982 Triple Crown matches, against Wales. Ireland's scrum half Robbie McGrath sweeps the ball away to his backs, with John O'Driscoll, Fergus Slattery and Willie Duggan (partly hidden) on hand to offer support if necessary.

old hands producing their best form, and Keane certainly gave proof that he still had something to offer.

The team to meet Wales, for a game scheduled for Dublin on January 16th, was not selected following the trial, the selectors wisely deciding to wait until a fortnight before the match.

Two days after Christmas, there occurred an event that was to have major repercussions. Campbell decided that it was time to make his return and he played for his club against Bective Rangers. Two of the five Ireland selectors, Kevin Flynn and Roly Meates, attended the game, as did coach Tom Kiernan, and they saw Campbell give a five star display. Although that was the only game he played before the team to meet Wales was announced, Campbell was chosen for the international. There was one other change behind the scrum. Terry Kennedy, who had played on the left wing against Australia, was recovering from a broken leg. So five of the backs were retained, with Campbell coming in for Ward and Moss Finn, from Constitution, replacing Kennedy. Finn had won one cap three years previously against England and had had quite a lot of injury problems in the interim; indeed they persisted into the current season and he missed two of the games Munster played. In the pack, John Cantrell was dropped from the hooking position and Ciaran Fitzgerald recalled and made captain. Gerry McLoughlin, from Shannon, ousted Mick Fitzpatrick at tight head prop, and Keane was brought back into the second row for Brendan Foley. Keane's partner was a youngster from the University College Club, Donal Lenihan who had made his debut against Australia and, although not very impressive, still held out immense promise, notably as a fine jumper in the line out, a chronic Irish need. Surprisingly the back row, so badly mauled against Australia, was retained en bloc.

The game against Wales had to be postponed for a week owing to the severe frost and snow which enveloped Britain and Ireland, and it was on January 23rd that Ireland faced Wales in Dublin. The day of reckoning had arrived and Ciaran Fitzgerald remembers it well.

'I felt that the Irish side's record was totally out of proportion to its ability and experience,' he told me. 'On a personal level, I was very pleased to be back in the team and honoured to be given the captaincy. The fact that the game was at home was a help, and I also felt that Wales had deteriorated a lot following the retirement of so many of the great players of the seventies. We had been very unlucky against them

Moss Keane, Ireland's veteran second row forward who made a triumphant return to the Ireland side against Wales, receives attention from Irish physiotherapist Joe Doran watched by Phil Orr (number 1), John O'Driscoll, Geoff Wheel of Wales and the referee John Anderson, of Scotland.

Ollie Campbell, who played such a big part in the destruction of Wales, lines up a kick watched by his scrum half Robbie McGrath.

Ireland's right wing Trevor Ringland scores his first try for Ireland, with Gareth Davies, the Welsh outside half, on his back after failing to stop him. David Irwin, the Irish centre, has his arms raised in acclamation.

the previous season. Tom Kiernan kept telling us that we had the ability to win this one, but he knew, as we all did, that it was a crucial match, not just in terms of the Triple Crown and Championship, but for the future, bearing in mind that we had so far lost seven successive games.'

Terry Holmes, the Welsh scrum half, goes over the Irish line for a Welsh try, as signalled by Referee John Anderson to the delight of the Welsh players.

Fitzgerald was, in fact, a truly splendid choice as captain of the side and there is no doubt his qualities of leadership were a very important factor in his selection over Cantrell, who had played well against Australia, one of the few who did.

Fitzgerald, a captain in the Irish Army, had led Connacht in the interprovincial series for two years, and had also captained Ireland 'B' against Scotland

in 1977. He is a sportsman of rounded talents, for he excelled at hurling and boxing before giving his full time to rugby. He joined St Mary's College club after being posted to Dublin.

His selection as captain of the side also maintained a quite remarkable sequence for his club who, of course, had also produced Tom Grace, Shay Deering and John Moloney in the late seventies. Four

captains from the same club in the space of six seasons is a tremendous tribute when one remembers that it was not until 1970 that they managed to get a man on the Ireland side for the first time.

Ireland, in fact, made a very hesitant start against Wales and were 9-4 down in the first half. Indeed Wales had lost a golden chance to get a try. Then the balance changed dramatically. Trevor Ringland

Ollie Campbell, the determination reflected on his face, puts in a clearance.

Ireland's left wing Moss Finn crosses the Welsh line for his second and Ireland's third, try of the match.

had scored Ireland's four points which came when they were badly needed. But Terry Holmes had scored a try for Wales which had been converted by their full back, Gwyn Evans, who also kicked a penalty goal.

The Irish forwards, superbly led by Fitzgerald, took over and Campbell turned on the magic. He made a glorious break from a scrum and paved the way for Moss Finn to get a try. From that point on, there was but one side in it.

In contrast to the lethargy revealed against Australia, the Irish pack completely dominated in every phase and the line out work of Keane and Lenihan gave Ireland a marked edge in a vital area. Campbell was masterly at out half and though losing both centres through injury, Ireland continued to prosper. Campbell made a great break to give Finn a second try early in the second period and Wales just could not answer the challenge; Ireland won 20-12. The crowd, so long starved of a victory, went wild

and immediately thoughts, not of wooden spoons, but of Triple Crowns began to exercise the minds of the Irish rugby public. They had seen a win on home soil for the first time in two years, with Wales again the victims of Irish tenacity.

If the public were talking in terms of the Triple Crown, Fitzgerald and Kiernan kept a much more balanced perspective. David Irwin had broken a leg against Wales, a misfortune that had brought Michael Kiernan into the centre, where he stayed for the remainder of the season; while Paul Dean, who had left the field in the game against Wales, recovered and was back in time for the visit to Twickenham. He had been replaced in the Welsh match by John Murphy, the reserve full back, and Murphy had played very well in his new role, giving the scoring pass to Finn for Ireland's third try.

'Obviously we were delighted to have got that win against Wales,' said Fitzgerald, 'but we knew facing England at Twickenham would be a very different proposition. Quite honestly there was no talk of the Triple Crown among the players, even if at the back of our minds we felt a win at Twickenham

The match against England at Twickenham. England
scrum half Steve Smith gets the ball away as Fergus Slattery

*closes in, with Willie Duggan and Peter Winterbottom
keeping a close watch on proceedings.*

would set us up nicely, as we had Scotland at home in the third match. Tom Kiernan deliberately stifled all talk of the Crown and the Championship. His attitude was one match at a time. He had been proved right in his previous assertions about the team being much better than their record, but one swallow does not make a summer. We went to Twickenham quite hopefully, but not with any degree of over-confidence. In many respects, I think our performance against England was the best we gave throughout the season.'

England suffered a big blow a few days before the game when their captain Bill Beaumont had to withdraw after receiving a kick on the head playing for Lancashire.

'That was obviously a set-back for England,' said Fitzgerald, 'but we did not feel it made our task very much easier. England had drawn with Scotland at Murrayfield, with the Scots getting a late penalty, and we knew England now retained very concrete hopes of winning the Championship. Remember, they still had the majority of the side that had done the Grand Slam in 1980.'

Fitzgerald stressed too that the Irish knew the English forwards would present greater problems than the Welsh. 'We knew this would be a game of a different nature,' he said. 'It was essential that we should match them up front, and we knew that. As things turned out, we did more. We were as good as them in the tight, after some initial difficulty, did well in the line out and what was the most important factor in my view, we beat them to the loose ball. We

Moss Keane breaks through the tackle of England prop Phil Blakeway.

Ireland's number eight Willie Duggan in possession with Gerry McLoughlin in support, as England's Maurice Colclough attempts to stop Duggan.

Ireland's full back Hugo MacNeill scores Ireland's first try at Twickenham and his third in international rugby. He is the only full back to have scored three tries for Ireland.

were arriving at the point of breakdown in a ratio of two to one and that gave us a great advantage. The backs too did very well, with Ollie Campbell again in top form. When stress was put on the defence, the backs tackled very effectively. In the end, we won by only a point, but I think most people agree that we were worth more than that, with England getting six points in the last minutes.'

Tries by Hugo MacNeill, his third for Ireland, and a memorable try from Gerry McLoughlin, paved the way for the Irish victory. This time the fluid back play that had characterised the game against Wales was not evident, but Ireland played well and with commendable common sense.

Now the Triple Crown loomed on the horizon, with Scotland to come a fortnight later at Lansdowne Road.

The whole of Ireland wanted to see that game, but

the Lansdowne Road ground holds only 50,000. The demand for tickets was unprecedented and the interest at fever pitch. What made the occasion unique was that Ireland had never won the Triple Crown at Lansdowne Road. Moreover, such had been the sequence of games in the past, combined with the fact that until the mid fifties Belfast was allocated a home game annually, that Ireland had never yet played for the Triple Crown at Lansdowne Road.

Kiernan now knew the two sides of the coaching coin and, drawing on his great experience as a player, worked hard to keep the game in perspective and to keep the players calm.

The night of the match against England, he called the players into a room at the team hotel and told them not to be carried away by the two wins. 'You will be heroes now with the journalists,' said Kiernan, 'but do not get a wrong sense of perspective because of it.'

'It was hard,' said Ciaran Fitzgerald, 'to keep our minds off the Triple Crown. We knew that the Irish public was expecting us to win, and that put additional pressure on us. But it was pressure we had to

Fergus Slattery beats England flanker Peter Winterbottom for possession with scrum half Robbie McGrath in support.

Trevor Ringland, the Ireland right wing, tries to break past England scrum half and captain Steve Smith (9) and hooker Peter Wheeler (2).

Fergus Slattery makes a valiant attempt to block down a kick by England left wing Mike Slemen. Centre Paul Dean is on Slattery's left.

live with. If we could not come to terms with the situation, then we would not deserve to win the Triple Crown.'

The mood of expectancy was patently obvious from the moment one entered Lansdowne Road on the afternoon of February 20th.

The day was dull and rather blustery and the match itself was far from being a classic. From the outset, the Scots conceded penalties and they paid the price as Campbell extracted the full benefit. He called the tune behind the scrum and scored all Ireland's 21 points in a 21–12 win. He kicked six penalty goals and dropped a goal. Scotland scored a very good try in the first half, but it was not their match and their captain Andy Irvine had a completely off day with his place kicking.

Ciaran Fitzgerald commented: 'We did not go out to play 10-man rugby, even allowing for the importance of the occasion, and I must stress that Tom

Kiernan has never instructed us to do that. On the contrary, Kiernan is the most flexible man in that regard and leaves matters very much to the players, in the belief and confidence that, if they are good enough to play for Ireland, they are perceptive enough to do the right things at the right time. In many ways the pattern of the match was set early on when Scotland conceded penalties from an early stage. I know it was not a great match.'

It was, however, a memorable occasion, and when referee Clive Norling blew the final whistle, the pitch was invaded and the players carried off shoulder high. Some were lucky enough to get to the sanctuary of the dressing room quickly, but Campbell had a difficult time as all of Ireland wanted to shake his hand. 'There's only one Ollie Campbell,' went the chant and at that time, Ireland was Campbell's kingdom.

'We had won the Triple Crown and the Championship,' said Ciaran Fitzgerald, 'but one more job remained to be done. We had to go to France for the final match, and there was a month between that game and our win over Scotland. It was essential that we keep a proper sense of balance.'

106

'On a plate' are probably the sentiments of Ireland's second row forward Moss Keane as he delivers the ball to scrum half Robbie McGrath. Keane was playing in his forty-first international for Ireland.

France had been having a very lean time and had lost all three games when they faced Ireland. The French selectors decided to bring back the old campaigners in the pack, in an effort to soften up the Irish who went to Paris seeking their first win there in 10 years.

On the eve of the match, Ireland suffered a great blow when Willie Duggan had to withdraw because of a damaged wrist. Ireland moved John O'Driscoll from flank to number eight and called in Ronan Kearney of Wanderers on the flank. It was not a happy omen for the game that offered Ireland the

chance to do the Grand Slam for the first time since the heady days of 1948, only the second time in their history. And Ireland failed in their objective, for the French at last got things right and won a worthy victory by 22 points to nine. While the final tally was not really reflective of the general trend, with France scoring in the final minutes, neither was there any doubt that, on the day, Ireland did not deserve to win.

Duggan was a considerable loss, but Fitzgerald does not believe it cost Ireland the match. 'Of course we missed Duggan and his tremendous experience and he was very badly missed in the line out. But, even allowing for that, we did not really play well in the game. In the other matches we took the chances when they came; against France we did not. The

French team,' he added, 'was picked to do a job. They set out to disrupt us and succeeded to a large degree. I felt at half time that we still had a hope of winning, but just after the interval we missed a great chance to score a try. From that point on, the French got on top. In contrast to us, they took their chances and, as so often happens, it went on from there.

'But all in all we had a very good year. It would have been nice to end it with the Grand Slam, but the Triple Crown and the Championship are a fair return for the work put in, not just by the players, but by Tom Kiernan and the selectors.' Fitzgerald does not subscribe to the view that the Irish pack is now too old to go on for another year, even though he and Lenihan are the only members of it under 30.

'I think all the members of that pack still have something to give Ireland,' was Fitzgerald's final comment on the year that Ireland came out of the wilderness, and on the men who brought the Crown and the Championship back when least expected.

There is no doubt that the season of 1982 was one of the high points in the rugby history of Ireland. There have been times when things were not good and, no doubt, such will be the case again, but the essential character of Irish rugby has always come through. That is the heritage passed on by George Hall Stack and the men who played in the first Ireland side to take the field. Unity, fraternity, sportsmanship and a great care for the ethos of rugby football have always been inherent in the game in Ireland. In the final analysis, they are no bad memorial to the men who started it all, over 100 years ago.

The Ireland back row that helped win the Triple Crown in 1982. John O'Driscoll (with ball) in action, supported by Willie Duggan and Fergus Slattery.

Ireland had never won the Triple Crown on their home ground at Lansdowne Road. Here Ireland captain Ciaran

Fitzgerald leads his side out for the game against Scotland, and his face clearly shows the tension of the occasion.

Ollie Campbell, who kicked a record twenty-one points in the match, about to take one of his successful kicks at goal.

Ireland's captain Ciaran Fitzgerald makes a typically determined drive for the line with prop Gerry McLoughlin in close support on his right.

Ciaran Fitzerald passes the ball to Moss Keane with Robbie McGrath and Donal Lenihan in close support.

Ollie Campbell gets his kick away as a Scotland forward attempts to charge it down.

Heroes to a man. Ireland's captain Ciaran Fitzgerald and wing Moss Finn eventually get off the field after Ireland won the Triple Crown.

Fergus Slattery, with Ollie Campbell in support, makes a break for the French line in the match at Parc des Princes when France foiled Ireland's hopes of the Grand Slam.

The 1982 Ireland team: Triple Crown winners and International Champions. Back row (l. to r.): A. Richards (touch judge), F. Slattery, G. McLoughlin, J. O'Driscoll, D. Lenihan, M. Keane, W. Duggan, H. MacNeill, P. Orr, C. Norling (referee), K. Rowlands (touch judge). In front: M. Kiernan, P. Dean, O. Campbell, C. Fitzgerald (capt.), J. Moore (President, I.R.F.U.), M. Finn, R. McGrath, K. Crossan. Insets (l. to r.): J. Murphy (played against Wales), T. Ringland (played against Wales and England), D. Irwin (played against Wales).

Ireland's leading cap winners from 1875 to 1982.

M. Gibson 69
W. J. McBride 63
F. Slattery 56
T. Kiernan 54
J. Kyle 46
K. Kennedy 45
G. Stephenson 42
N. A. Murphy 41
N. Henderson 40
R. McLoughlin 40
M. Keane 43
S. Millar 37
R. Kavanagh 35
W. Mulcahy 35
P. Orr 35
E. O'D. Davy 34
W. Duggan 33
C. Pedlow 30
G. Hamlet 30
E. Crawford 30
J. D. Clinch 30
J. L. Farrell 29
G. Wood 29
A. O'Reilly 29
M. Sugden 28
J. McCarthy 28
L. Magee 27
R. Dawson 27
M. Molloy 27
J. Moloney 27
R. Young 26
G. Beamish 25
K. Mullen 25
J. Walsh 25
B. Bresnihan 25
A. Duggan 25
T. Grace 25
B. McGann 25
S. McKinney 25

Ireland's International record against all countries.

	P.	W.	D.	L.
v. England	94	33	8	53
v. Scotland	92	42	4	46
v. Wales	84	28	5	51
v. France	55	24	4	27
v. New Zealand	9	0	1	8
v. S. Africa	10	1	1	8
v. Australia	9	6	0	3
v. Romania	1	0	1	0
v. Argentina	5	2	1	2
v. President's XV	1	0	1	0 (X)

(X) *Caps awarded for match v. President's XV in centenary season 1974-75.*

Ireland's most capped players in each position.

Full Back: T. Kiernan (54) *equals World Record*
Wing: T. O. Grace and A. Duggan (25)
Centre: M. Gibson (40)
Outside Half: J. Kyle (46)
Scrum Half: M. Sugden (28)
Prop: R. McLoughlin (40)
Hooker: K. Kennedy (45) *World Record*
Second Row: W. J. McBride (63) *World Record*
Flank Forward: F. Slattery (56) *World Record*
Number Eight: W. Duggan (31)

NOTE: Gibson also won 25 caps at outside half and four on the wing for a total of 69, to make him the world's most capped player.
Duggan also won two caps as a flank forward.
W. J. McBride played in a record 17 tests for the Lions and made five Lions tours, as did Gibson, which is also a record.

Most points in International rugby: T. J. Kiernan (158)

Most points in a Championship in a season: S. O. Campbell (46) *in season 1978–79 and in season 1981–82*

Most points for Ireland on overseas tour: S. O. Campbell (60) *in Australia in 1979*

Most points in any match on tour: S. O. Campbell (19) *Australia, first test Brisbane in 1979*; A. Ward (19) *Australian Capital Territory in Canberra in 1979*

Most tries in an international: Three: R. Montgomery *v. Wales at Birkenhead, March 1887*; J. P. Quinn, *v. France in Cork, 1913*; E. O'D. Davy, *v. Scotland at Murrayfield, 1930*; S. Byrne, *v. Scotland at Murrayfield, 1953*

Highest try scorer for Ireland: A. Duggan (11)

T. J. Kiernan has captained Ireland on most occasions (24)

The following Fathers and Sons have played for Ireland. *In each instance the years of first and last caps are given.*

A. D. Clinch (Dublin University and Wanderers) 1885–97
J. D. Clinch (Dublin University and Wanderers) 1924–32

W. Collis (Wanderers) 1884
W. R. Collis (Harlequins and K.C.H.) 1924–26

M. P. Crowe (Blackrock College and Lansdowne) 1929–34
J. Crowe (U.C.D.) 1974

G. Collopy (Bective Rangers) 1891–92
W. P. Collopy (Bective Rangers) 1914–24
R. Collopy (Bective Rangers) 1923–25

S. J. Deering (Bective Rangers) 1935–37
S. M. Deering (Garryowen and St. Mary's College) 1974–78

T. R. Hewitt (Queen's University) 1924–26
D. Hewitt (Queen's University and Instonians) 1958–65

S. T. Irwin (Queen's University) 1900–03
J. W. S. Irwin (Queen's University and N.I.F.C.) 1938–39

N. F. Murphy (Constitution) 1930–33
N. A. Murphy (Constitution) 1958–69

P. F. Murray (Wanderers) 1927–33
J. Murray (U.C.D.) 1963

H. R. McKibbin (Queen's University and Instonians) 1938–39
C. H. McKibbin (Instonians) 1976
A. R. McKibbin (Instonians and London Irish) 1977–80

F. Schute (Wanderers) 1878–79
F. G. Schute (Dublin University) 1913

The following is a list of brothers who have played for Ireland.

Three brothers

E. Doran (Lansdowne) 1890
G. P. Doran (Lansdowne) 1899–1904
B. R. Doran (Lansdowne) 1900–02

A. J. Forrest (Wanderers) 1880–83
E. G. Forrest (Wanderers) 1889–97
H. Forrest (Wanderers) 1893

T. A. Harvey (Dublin University) 1900–03
A. D. Harvey (Wanderers) 1903–05
F. M. W. Harvey (Wanderers) 1907–11

F. S. Hewitt (Instonians) 1926–27
T. R. Hewitt (Queen's University) 1924–26
V. A. Hewitt (Instonians) 1935–36

W. E. Johnstone (Dublin University) 1884
R. W. Johnstone (Dublin University) 1890
R. Johnstone (Wanderers) 1893

S. McVicker (Queen's University) 1922
J. McVicker (Collegians) 1924–30
H. McVicker (Army) 1927–28

D. F. Moore (Wanderers) 1883–84
F. W. Moore (Wanderers) 1884–86
C. M. Moore (Dublin University) 1887–88

J. Pedlow (Bessbrook) 1882–84
T. B. Pedlow (Queen's University) 1889
R. Pedlow (Bessbrook) 1891

D. J. Ross (Belfast Albion) 1884–86
J. P. Ross (Lansdowne) 1885–86
J. F. Ross (N.I.F.C.) 1886

T. Smyth (Malone) 1908–12
W. S. Smyth (Collegians) 1910–20
P. J. Smyth (Collegians) 1911

C. Glynn Allen (Derry and Liverpool) 1896–99
C. Elliott Allen (Derry and Liverpool) 1900–07

George R. Beamish (Coleraine and R.A.F.) 1925–33
Charles E. Beamish (Coleraine and R.A.F.) 1935–36

H. Brown (Windsor) 1877
T. Brown (Windsor) 1877

M. J. Bulger (Dublin University and Lansdowne) 1899
L. Q. Bulger (Dublin University and Lansdowne) 1896–98

F. Byrne (U.C.D.) 1962
S. J. Byrne (Lansdowne and U.C.D.) 1953–55

W. P. Collopy (Bective Rangers) 1914–24
R. Collopy (Bective Rangers) 1923–25

M. P. Crowe (Lansdowne) 1929–34
P. Crowe (Blackrock College) 1935

M. Deering (Bective Rangers) 1929
S. J. Deering (Bective Rangers) 1935–37

C. J. Dick (Ballymena) 1961–63
J. S. Dick (Queen's University) 1962

M. Doyle (Cambridge University and Blackrock College) 1965–68
T. Doyle (Wanderers) 1968

C. Feighery (Lansdowne) 1972
T. Feighery (St. Mary's College) 1977

E. Galbraith (Dublin University) 1875
R. Galbraith (Dublin University) 1875–77

W. Gardiner (N.I.F.C.) 1892–98
F. T. Gardiner (N.I.F.C.) 1900–09

L. H. Gwynn (Dublin University) 1894–98
A. P. Gwynn (Dublin University) 1895

J. Heron (N.I.F.C.) 1877–79
W. T. Heron (N.I.F.C.) 1880

L. Hunter (Civil Service) 1968
W. R. Hunter (C.I.Y.M.S.) 1962–66

P. Kavanagh (U.C.D.) 1952
R. Kavanagh (U.C.D. and Wanderers) 1953–61

F. Kennedy (Wanderers) 1880–82
J. M. Kennedy (Wanderers) 1882–84

J. Lyttle (N.I.F.C.) 1889–94
J. H. Lyttle (N.I.F.C.) 1894–99

L. M. Magee (Bective Rangers and London Irish) 1895–1904
J. T. Magee (Bective Rangers) 1895

E. H. McIlwaine (N.I.F.C.) 1895
J. E. McIlwaine (N.I.F.C.) 1897–99

H. R. McKibbin (Queen's University and Instonians) 1938–39
D. E. McKibbin (Instonians) 1950–51

C. H. McKibbin (Instonians) 1976
A. R. McKibbin (Instonians and London Irish) 1977–80

R. J. McLoughlin (Gosforth and Blackrock College) 1962–75
F. McLoughlin (Northern) 1976

R. B. Montgomery (Queen's University and Cambridge University) 1887–92
A. Montgomery (N.I.F.C.) 1895

H. Moore (Windsor) 1876–77
W. Moore (Queen's University) 1878

B. O'Driscoll (Manchester) 1971
J. O'Driscoll (London Irish) 1978–82

K. P. O'Flanagan (London Irish) 1947
M. O'Flanagan (Lansdowne) 1949

T. O. Pike (Lansdowne) 1927–28
V. J. Pike (Lansdowne) 1931–34

M. Ryan (Rockwell College) 1897–1904
J. Ryan (Rockwell College) 1897–1904

D. Scott (Malone) 1961–62
R. D. Scott (Queen's University) 1967–68

Donal Spring (Dublin University and Lansdowne) 1978–81
Dick Spring (Lansdowne) 1979

G. V. Stephenson (Queen's University and United Services) 1920–30
H. W. Stephenson (United Services) 1922–28

F. O. Stoker (Wanderers) 1886–89
E. W. Stoker (Wanderers) 1988

R. B. Walkington (N.I.F.C.) 1875–82
D. B. Walkington (Dublin University) 1887–91

Joseph Wallace (Wanderers) 1902–06
James Wallace (Wanderers) 1904

W. A. Wallis (Wanderers) 1881–83
A. K. Wallis (Wanderers) 1892–93

Fergus Slattery and Noel Murphy, two of the greatest flank forwards to play for Ireland. Slattery is the world's most capped flanker, an honour he took over from Murphy.

Seamus Deering, whose father and uncle played for Ireland, leads out the side against New Zealand in Dublin in 1978. Deering succeeded his two St. Mary's College clubmates Tom Grace and John Moloney as Ireland captain, the first time that the same club provided three successive Ireland captains.

Willie Duggan, Ireland's most capped number eight, takes on the French defence.

Tom Kiernan played his last game for Ireland against Scotland in 1973 and here is seen scoring a try in his last international, one of two he scored for his country in fifty-four appearances. He has captained Ireland on a record twenty-four occasions, and is also Ireland's leading points scorer in international rugby with one hundred and fifty-eight points.

127

*Tony Ward (left) discusses tactics with Ireland's most
capped player Mike Gibson during a training session at
Lansdowne Road.*